S. E Cottam

A Lantern for Lent

Brief Instructions on Biblical Subjects

S. E Cottam

A Lantern for Lent
Brief Instructions on Biblical Subjects

ISBN/EAN: 9783741193378

Manufactured in Europe, USA, Canada, Australia, Japa

Cover: Foto ©Lupo / pixelio.de

Manufactured and distributed by brebook publishing software (www.brebook.com)

S. E Cottam

A Lantern for Lent

A Lantern for Lent

Brief Instructions on Biblical Subjects for the

Forty Days of Lent

By the Rev.

S. E. Cottam, M.A.

Exeter College, Oxford

"Thy Word is a Lantern unto my feet, and a Light unto my paths."—*Psalm* cxix. 105.

London

IMPORTED BY
Thomas Whittaker,
2 & 3 Bible House,
NEW YORK.

:cadilly, W.

"BLESSED LORD, WHO HAST CAUSED ALL HOLY SCRIPTURES TO BE WRITTEN FOR OUR LEARNING; GRANT THAT WE MAY IN SUCH WISE HEAR THEM, READ, MARK, LEARN, AND INWARDLY DIGEST THEM, THAT BY PATIENCE, AND COMFORT OF THY HOLY WORD, WE MAY EMBRACE, AND EVER HOLD FAST THE BLESSED HOPE OF EVERLASTING LIFE, WHICH THOU HAST GIVEN US IN OUR SAVIOUR JESUS CHRIST. *Amen.*"

N.B.—It is suggested that this Collect be said before and after every Meditation.

DEDICATED

BY KIND PERMISSION
TO
THE RIGHT REV. MANDELL CREIGHTON,

LORD BISHOP OF LONDON.

by Google

Introduction.

NOWADAYS the Bible is read little, studied less, yet it might be made exceedingly helpful as a book of devotion—one of the best. Few can say with the Psalmist, "Thy Word is a lantern unto my feet, and a light unto my paths," and of few can it be said, "From a child hast thou known the Holy Scriptures." Yet how useful they are "for instruction in righteousness." The other day I heard a Sunday School teacher observe that she knew as much of the Bible as *any* clergyman! What an opinion she must have had of her own attainments, or of the general ignorance of the clergy!

The Bible in Christian times seems, roughly speaking, to have passed through three stages. First, it was comparatively unknown for lack of copies; then it was opened to the multitude by the invention of printing, to be either carefully studied, as by Bunyan in the construction of his "Pilgrim's Progress," or to be perverted in the interests of heresy and schism.

> "In religion
> What damned error but some sober brow
> Will bless it and approve it with a text,
> Hiding the grossness with fair ornament?"
> "*Merchant of Venice*," iii. 2.

Thirdly, it has passed into disuse, being fixed in the window on a small table, covered with an antimacassar and surmounted by a flower-pot, to be at last dismissed to the pawnshop, where it has become a glut in the market.

A fair general acquaintance with the Book of Life should form part of the education of every one. But folks should not be left entirely to the light of their own understanding, or the chances are they will go wrong. The Church having written the Bible, and preserved it, has alone the right of interpretation. With this end in view she has drawn up Creeds and Services, selected Psalms and Lessons, Epistles and Gospels, that her members may have a comprehensive idea of its contents and principles.

The aim of this present little work is to set forth in outline a few brief studies for use during Lent. It is believed that a great many people, with the very best of intentions, are utterly at a loss how to keep Lent, and that a far larger number do not get beyond small negative duties, such as leaving off tobacco or taking no sugar in their tea. It is therefore proposed that a systematic study of Scripture be made a special feature in the religious exercises of Lent, as a help in the development of the spiritual life. A temporary Guild might be formed, called the Guild of the Holy Writings, with the one simple rule, easily kept, that those who joined should read carefully the daily portion selected. Weekly meetings might be held for encouragement and for instruction on the lines laid down, and one or two examinations as a test of results. It is hoped that the plan on which the passages have been chosen may prove suggestive both to the beginner in pointing the road to progress as well as to the advanced student in setting forth fresh combinations.

The different periods of forty days have been taken as the backbone of the scheme. Each period seems to suggest a distinct thought of its own; to each thought has been allotted a week, and each has been emphasized by other examples, sufficiently numerous to fill up the days. Our Lord in the wilderness suggests Temptation;—Jonah at Nineveh, Repentance;—Elijah on Mount Horeb, Meditation;—the spies in Palestine, Investigation;—Moses in the mount, Revelation;—the waters of the Flood, Punishment; and this brings us as far as Holy Week, when the life of our Blessed Lord will be followed throughout the history of the last days, according to the most approved harmony of events. To this notes are added on Easter and on the Great Forty Days. May the good God teach us to delight in the wisdom of the Holy Writings.

Contents.

Chap. I. Temptation   PAGE

    OF CHRIST,—40 DAYS 1
    OF JOB 4
    OF ABRAHAM 7
    OF GOD 10

„ **II. Repentance**

    OF NINEVEH,—40 DAYS 14
    OF ESAU 18
    OF ACHAN   22
    OF DAVID   25
    OF PETER   29
    OF THIEF 33
    OF CORINTHIAN   37

„ **III. Meditation**

    OF ELIJAH,—40 DAYS ... 41
    OF ISAAC 45
    OF SAMUEL 49
    OF ASAPH ... 53
    OF HEZEKIAH 58
    OF CHRIST 62
    OF TIMOTHY   66

Chap. IV. Investigation

	PAGE
OF SPIES,—40 DAYS	70
OF GOD	74
OF MAN	78
OF NATURE	82
OF SCRIPTURE	86
OF HISTORY	90
OF HEART	94

" V. Revelation

OF LAW,—40 DAYS	98
OF GOD	102
OF SIN	106
OF LOVE	111
OF THE SON	116
OF REAL PRESENCE	120
OF HEAVEN	124

" VI. Punishment

OF WORLD,—40 DAYS	128
OF ADAM	132
OF JOSEPH	137
OF PHARAOH	141
OF ISRAEL	145
OF BETHEL	149
OF CHRIST	153

		PAGE
CHAP. VII. **Holy Week.**		
	DAY OF—HOSANNAS	157
	PARABLES	162
	QUESTIONS	166
	RETREAT	171
	COMMANDMENT ...	175
	DEATH	179
	SILENCE	183

APPENDIX.

NOTE I.	EASTER	...	188
„ II.	THE GREAT FORTY DAYS	...	188

A Lantern for Lent.

CHAPTER I., Sec. 1.

Ash Wednesday.

THE TEMPTATION OF CHRIST.
Matt. iv. 1 to 12.

Notes :—

1. The temptations were continuous during the forty days (Luke iv. 2), but the three last only are given. Beside these there were many others afterwards, for Christ, at the end of His career, said that His disciples had continued with Him in His temptations (Luke xxii. 28). Our temptations also are lifelong. But probably there will be some event, or course of events, which will be the turning point, after which we shall go in the main right or wrong.

2. S. Luke alters the order of the last two temptations for literary reasons. The order of S. Matthew seems to be the historical one, to judge

by the close connecting links that are given, the most important of which are—

(*a*) "If Thou be the Son of God," according to the declaration of the voice at Thy Baptism.

(*b*) "If Thou (really) be the Son of God," according to that declaration and Thy own claim just made.

(*c*) "Get thee hence," a mark of dismissal, closely connected with the third temptation.

3. The nature of the temptations.

(*a*) A temptation of the flesh, to want of faith or trust.

(*b*) A temptation of the devil, to pride, presumption, rashness.

(*c*) A temptation of the world, to unlawful ambition.

The third was the most subtle of all the temptations. One little act of worship, without further trouble, would secure the final end of Redemption. The devil, who is the "prince," and even the "god" of this world, offers, in return for a small act of homage, to abdicate in favour of our Lord: he will no longer harass mankind: the purpose of God will be fulfilled, but not in God's way. It was a most attractive and plausible proposition, appealing to our Lord not only as the obscure Carpenter of Nazareth, but also as Son of God.

In these three temptations the devil probably presented himself successively in the character of a traveller, a priest, and a king.

4. Methods of resisting temptation.

(*a*) Do it at once, without parley. "Resist the devil, and he will flee from you" (James iv. 7).

(*b*) Make the sign of the Cross.

> "At the sign of triumph
> Satan's host doth flee."
> —*Baring Gould.*

(*c*) Pray—" From all the deceits of the world, the flesh, and the devil, good Lord, deliver us" (*Litany*).

" Lord, we beseech Thee, grant Thy people grace to withstand the temptations of the world, the flesh, and the devil, and with pure hearts and minds to follow Thee, the only God; through Jesus Christ our Lord. Amen" (*Collect for 18th Sunday after Trinity*).

5. These are the three giants we have constantly to fight. The familiar fairy tale of "Jack, the Giant Killer," contains a mighty truth.

6. It is a comfort to know that there is no sin in the experience of a temptation. Our Lord was tempted, but remained sinless. The sin comes in by yielding. Temptations are necessary as discipline, for correcting our faults, and building up our character. S. James says, "Count it all joy, my brethren, when ye fall into manifold temptations (or trials), knowing that the proof of your faith worketh patience" (i. 2). And again, "Blessed is the man that endureth temptation: for when he hath been approved he shall receive the crown of life, which the Lord promised to them that love Him" (i. 12).

CHAPTER I., Sec. 2.

Thursday.

THE TEMPTATION OF JOB.

Job i. 1 to ii. 11.

NOTES:—

1. Three dire temptations came to Job—through his property, in the loss of his possessions; through his affections, in the loss of his sons and daughters; and through his health, in the sore boils which covered him from the sole of his foot to the crown of his head—yet he retained his integrity. It is said that a friend once came to a rich man, and asked if he did not find it difficult to serve God with so much wealth, and he replied, "No; I find God in everything." It happened that he lost all his property, and the same friend, coming to him again, asked if he did not find it difficult to serve God in his poverty, and he replied, "No; I find everything in God." This story sums up the lesson of the life of Job.

2. In our greatest grief we have that comfortable word—"The Lord gave, and the Lord hath taken away; blessed be the name of the Lord" (*Burial Office.* See also Job xix. 25-27).

3. From chap. i. 5 we see that Job lived in a continual state of preparation. Every day he sought absolution.

4. From chap. ii. 9 we see that, though Job was an upright and almost a perfect man, one who feared God and eschewed evil, he had a bad and foolish wife; which should warn us that a great many people are not intended to marry, a different ideal being set before them, and that those who think of marrying should do it more carefully, according to the rules of choice laid down in the Marriage Service, which embody the advice of the Church given and explained in chap. iii., sec. 2.

5. Since Job's restoration was as remarkable as his calamity, it may be observed—(*a*) That the number of his sons and daughters was the same as before (xlii. 13), *i.e.*, really doubled like the rest of his property, for the first family, though dead, were still alive in another state of existence, which we may take as an intimation of the doctrine of the immortality of the soul, and may compare it with the confidence and persistence of the child in Wordsworth's exquisite poem, " We are seven."

(*b*) Job was blessed in his daughters, as far as we can tell from the significance of their names—Jemima, Kezia, and Keren-happuch. Two were famed for their transcendent beauty, and the other for the sweetness of her disposition. Jemima—handsome as the day; or, perhaps, gentle as a dove.

Kezia = cassia, an aromatic plant, used as an ingredient of the holy anointing oil (Ex. xxx. 24), and mentioned as a symbol of the fragrance of the royal Messiah (Psalm xlv. 9). Keren-happuch = horn of stibium, a product used in the east by ladies for darkening their eyes to improve their appearance. Job's daughter, however, was so beautiful that she did not need this artificial assistance, so glorious and splendid was God's gift: a distinct hint to the women of to-day not to use curling irons, and not to put on false hair or rouge, but to be content with natural beauty simply adorned.

CHAPTER I., Sec. 3.

𝔉riday.

THE TEMPTATION OF ABRAHAM.
Gen. xxii. 1 to 20.

Notes :—

1. We all like to locate events—the field of Waterloo, the house where Shakespeare was born—where, then, did this striking scene take place ? Was it upon the temple hill at Jerusalem, or on Mount Gerizim, situated about the middle of Palestine ? The one is the tradition of the Jews, the other of the Samaritans. The latter is probably right, for Abraham "lifted up his eyes and saw the place afar off," which would be impossible at Jerusalem. Moreover, the temple was built on Mount Moriah (2 Chron. iii. 1), while Isaac was taken to a mountain in the land of Moriah.

2. We need not trouble ourselves about the supposed moral difficulty in the command to sacrifice a human life; like other difficulties it was overcome by the splendid faith of Abraham, shown in his promise to the young men, that after he and his son had worshipped *they* would return.

3. Isaac carrying the wood is a type of Christ carrying His Cross—" He, bearing His Cross, went forth " (John xix. 17), which is the incident of the second of the so-called Stations of the Cross.

4. Isaac, though bound for convenience, was a willing victim. The words that Tennyson wrote of Jephthah's daughter may be appropriated to him—

> "Strength came to him that equalled his desire:
> How beautiful a thing it was to die
> For God and for his sire."

Of all the pictures of this scene the one at the Academy, St. Petersburg, by a Russian artist, is far away the most beautiful. Those in which the face of the boy is hidden are absurd, for the artist thereby acknowledges his own inability to show us how he looked at the supreme moment of his life. According to tradition, Isaac was twelve years old at this time.

5. The day of Christ, (see John viii. 56), which Abraham rejoiced to see, was the birth, in his family, of the great Deliverer, to Whom he looked forward, and in Whom all the nations of the world were to be blessed. Also, it was the day of the Resurrection, for the doctrine of the Resurrection was added to his creed, when "in a figure" he received back Isaac from the dead (Heb. xi. 19). This is what S. Paul means when he says that the Gospel was preached beforehand to him (Gal. iii. 8).

6. We rightly lay a good deal of stress on the

The Temptation of Abraham. 9

expression, "the God of Abraham," because it was first in Abraham that faith came into such prominence, and it is a common faith that binds us together in the great family of the spiritual Israel, even the Holy Catholic Church (Rom. iv. 16). Faith is stronger than natural relationship, therefore Abraham sacrificed his son; therefore the Catholic Church superseded the Jewish Church; therefore we are called on to leave everything, even our husbands and wives, for the sake of Christ (Matt. xix. 29). See, for the other aspect of this expression, chap. vii., sec. 3.

CHAPTER I., Sec. 4.

Saturday.

THE TEMPTATION OF GOD.

Exodus xvi. 1 to 16, and xvii. 1 to 8.

Notes :—

1. The day of the striking of the rock is the well-known "day of temptation in the wilderness," referred to in the Venite (Psalm xcv.) as a warning to us not to harden our hearts, as the Israelites did on that occasion.

2. The strange expression, " to tempt God," is explained by such passages as Psalm lxxviii. 57, where an alternative word is provided, rendered by "provoked" in the A. V. and by "displeased" in the Prayer Book. So Scripture interprets itself, one writer providing the key to open the locked meaning of another writer. The longsuffering of God is terminable. If we go on still in our wickedness, patience will give place to punishment. The Almighty knows exactly how long to wait, and when to inflict a sharp correction. The word "displease" is better than the word "provoke," for one conveys

the idea of tenderness, while the other rather suggests to our minds irritation, which would be unworthy of God. The Holy Spirit of God is first "grieved" (Eph. iv. 30), then "resisted" (Acts vii. 51), then "quenched" (1 Thess. v. 19), and lastly "blasphemed" (Mark iii. 29).

3. S. Paul speaks of tempting Christ (1 Cor. x. 9), and refers to the Israelites murmuring against the manna; while S. Luke, in telling the story of Ananias and Sapphira, speaks of tempting the Holy Ghost (Acts v. 9).

4. The manna, the bread that saved their lives when they were hungry, is a type of the Bread of Life given at Communion. And the water that saved their lives when they were thirsty is a type of the Water of Life sprinkled at Baptism.

5. There was a tradition among the Jews that the rock which Moses struck followed the camp through the wilderness, and that there always issued from it a stream of fresh water. S. Paul refers to this tradition in 1 Cor. x. 4, and uses it as an allegorical type of Christ. The same idea is contained in Isaiah xxvi. 4, marg., on which Toplady built his beautiful hymn, "Rock of ages, cleft for me." Many a priest would be astonished at the fact that not ten per cent. of the children in his school could explain the title, "Rock of Ages." Yet it is so. The idea is strength. Thus we have Psalm xcv. 1, "The *rock* of our salvation," translated in the Prayer

Book, "The *strength* of our salvation." Again in Psalm xviii. 1, the LORD is called " my strength," and in verse 2 " my rock." Yet again, in Psalm xix. 14, the Hebrew of the margin " rock " is rendered in the text " strength."

It will be remembered that when the side of Jesus was cleft by the spear of Longinus there came forth blood and water, which are again types of the two Sacraments.

In hymn 128, A. & M., " The Lamb's high banquet called to share," there is in verse 2 an allusion to the blood as the " precious blood," in the first edition it was " crimson blood," while Dr. Neale rendered the original Latin more faithfully by "roseate blood," for the blood was the pale pink blood of an exhausted body; our Lord's suffering was extreme.

6. Comparing the account of the second smitten rock in Num. xx. it will be seen that Moses was one of those who tempted, provoked, or displeased God, so that he was severely punished in not being allowed to enter the Promised Land. In the Church of the Monastery La Caridad at Seville hangs Murillo's great picture of this great scene.

7. The temptation of God may be understood in the double sense of man tempting God and God tempting man. Both these senses are brought together in James i. 13 : " God cannot be tempted with evil, neither tempteth He any man." Here it would seem, at first sight, as if this sort of tempta-

tion, which God experiences and which God inflicts, was altogether denied as impossible, though in other places man is said to tempt God, and God is said to tempt man. The clue to the apparent contradiction is to be found in the small words "with evil." We have already seen how man tempts God; it is not with evil. Evil is not presented to the Almighty as an object of desire; such a thing would be utterly impossible. Again, when God tempts man, as He tempted Abraham, it is not with evil; He does not put evil before man as the devil does, tricked out with the charms of fascination, in the hope of his going wrong: such a thing would be likewise utterly impossible. When God is said to tempt it is in the sense of to try; God tried the faith of Abraham to see what it was worth. God does not entice to what is wrong; He rather tests what is good, to prove it, and to brace it with discipline.

CHAPTER II., Sec. 1.

First Sunday.

THE REPENTANCE OF NINEVEH.

Jonah III.

Notes :—

1. In considering the lessons of the story of Jonah and his journey to Nineveh, it is not necessary to trouble about the difficulties of the narrative, which may be well left to more advanced students.

2. Nineveh was the capital of Assyria, and apparently given up to all the vices of a great city, for the way of everyone was evil, and violence was in the hands of all (iii. 8). It was situated on the banks of the river Tigris. It was a great city, of three days' journey, *i.e.*, the circuit of the walls was about sixty miles, and its population is estimated at 600,000, a calculation based on the 60,000 children, the number of those who did not know the difference between their right and left hands (iv. 11). Its magnificence may be judged of by a visit to the British Museum, where the gigantic winged bulls are to be seen that were brought to England by Mr. Layard, and that

The Repentance of Nineveh. 15

made a greater impression upon me when I was a boy than any other objects in the Museum. It was one of the oldest and most famous cities of the ancient world, said to be larger than Babylon itself. It was destroyed about 606 B.C., after which it entirely disappeared from history, until it was dug up in 1845-50.

3. The repentance of Nineveh is referred to by our Lord in Matt. xii. 41, and the parallel passage in Luke xi. 32. The Ninevites, said He, would rise up in the Judgment against the men of His own generation, and condemn it, because they repented at the preaching of Jonah, while He, a greater Prophet, made no impression. A saying that we English should take home to ourselves, since such a large mass of the people have entirely lapsed from the Faith. It is no good to reckon ourselves as one of the three most religious nations of modern Europe. Comparisons of that sort should be made, not with the worst, nor even with the best of our fellow-men, but with the perfect Ideal set before us—and how far we come short of that! It is intended that this remark should apply also to individuals, as units of which the nation is composed.

4. The *people* of Nineveh believed, put on sackcloth, fasted, cried mightily unto God, turned over a new leaf, and so averted the threatened calamity from that generation. It shews what great results could be brought about by a national repentance,

what union and enthusiasm could accomplish, and what evils could be cured by their means. The expression "cried mightily" unto God, suggests with great force that we should put far more energy into our prayers.

5. The animals took part in the penance. The whole creation has in some mysterious way been affected by the Fall, for S. Paul says, in Rom. viii. 21, 22, that it groans and travails in pain together until now, but shall one day be delivered from the bondage of corruption.

6. God is said to have repented. This is merely an accommodation to human language; God cannot change: but since He determines to do one of two things, He may be said to repent of the other. If a man is wicked He determines to punish, but if that man repents He withdraws the threat; this is what is called God's repentance.

7. "The sign of the prophet Jonah" (Matt. xii. 40 and xvi. 4). Jonah was a type of Christ, and in particular of the Resurrection. We may trace the type in detail.

(*a*) Jonah preached repentance.
So did Christ (Mark i. 15; Luke xiii. 3).
(*b*) Jonah admitted Gentiles to the blessings of God,
Christ founded the *Catholic* Church for *all*.
(*c*) Jonah offered himself to death.
Christ died willingly (John x. 18).

The Repentance of Nineveh.

(*d*) Jonah came up from the storm after three days. Christ rose on the third day. The expression "after three days" (Mark viii. 31) is explained by the other way of saying the same thing, "on the third day" (Mark x. 34).

8. From 2 Kings xiv. 25 we learn that Jonah was born at Gath-hepher, a town in Zebulon, in Galilee, therefore the Pharisees were wrong when they said that no prophet came from that province (John vii. 52).

CHAPTER II., Sec. 2.

Monday.

THE REPENTANCE OF ESAU.

Gen. xxvii. to xxviii. 6.

Notes:—

1. At first sight the character of Jacob is not an attractive one, yet we must consider it here for a moment, because it serves to throw up the character of his elder brother by way of contrast. He was an abominable liar, a mean trickster, and when he was presented at the Egyptian Court he had to acknowledge that the days of the years of his life had been few and evil (Gen. xlvii. 9). But for all that we must not allow the vices to overshadow the virtues, and it was for these virtues that he was preferred to Esau. He had that love which hides a multitude of sins. He loved his mother, he loved his favourite wife, he loved his youngest son, and he loved his God, for it was his too eager desire to possess spiritual blessings that led him astray. His was a character of infinite possibilities for good, he had found the pearl of great price, he had bought the

ground in which the treasure lay hid, but he had not yet paid for it. Still these points in his favour do not excuse his vices, for which he had afterwards to undergo such severe discipline.

2. In marked contrast to this, is the character of Esau. He was a thoroughly worldly man who did not care two straws about spiritual things. He despised his birthright to the priesthood of the family, and bartered it away for a good dinner. He did not care for his father's blessing, except as it would bring him material prosperity. From the violent hatred he bore his brother he would have murdered him, and from spiteful malice to his parents he purposely married a wife of whom they did not approve. Jacob committed a few ugly sins, Esau plunged into a long course of action distasteful to God. It is true he was badly treated, but the bad treatment only developed the evil traits of a wicked heart, and was itself most severely punished.

3. To the question, " Did Esau repent ? " an affirmative answer must be given. The " bitter cry " was wrung from the depths of a sensitive heart, though the motive at that time was quite perverted. The blessing that he got, " the dew of Heaven from above," was, no doubt, a strong spiritual influence working for his conversion. In the very determination to murder his brother he showed considerable self-restraint and respect for his dying father, since

he fixed to do the deed, not at once, not directly his father died, not until the days of mourning were accomplished. Then on Jacob's return all angry feeling had passed away, he ran to meet him, he embraced him, he kissed him, he wept over him, and all this before he received the handsome present his brother offered. We cannot help liking the man, when he was converted, as he surely was at this time.

4. Whence then comes the impression that Esau died impenitent? It is from certain passages in the New Testament, (see Rom. ix. 13), where S. Paul writes of God, " Jacob have I loved, but Esau have I hated." It is a quotation from Malachi, where the prophet is explaining God's love for the Israelite nation by saying that He chose Jacob rather than Esau, and that He punished the wicked Edomites who were enemies to His people (Mal. i. 2, 3). Secondly, see Heb. xii. 16, 17, where the two events in the life of Esau are referred to. He is called " a profane person " for selling his birthright. Then comes the incident of the blessing, when his application for the blessing of the first-born was " rejected ": the blessing already bestowed on Jacob could not be revoked, and Esau " found no way to change his (father's) mind "—(see margin)—" though he sought it carefully with tears " and a bitter cry.

Thus we have got rid of a very mischievous interpretation. It would be a horrid nightmare to think that under some circumstances a man might wish to repent and could not. Every man can repent who sincerely wishes to do so, though it is impossible to alter the past. We can never get the blessings we've missed, but can secure others.

CHAPTER II., Sec. 3.

𝕿uesday.

THE REPENTANCE OF ACHAN.
Josh. vi. 17, 18, 19, and vii.

Notes :—

1. At the plunder of Jericho Achan took for himself what the people were commanded not to take, what, in fact, was consecrated to the service of God; therefore, when they began the siege of Ai, they were defeated with great slaughter; and, enquiring into the cause, discovered it was Achan's theft.

2. The Israelites themselves were somehow involved in the transaction, hence it was not unjust to punish them with defeat; and as Achan was the immediate cause of the death of those who fell, it was not unjust to punish him with death.

3. It is, of course, exceedingly difficult to trace effects to their remote causes as seen by God. It may appear to us unjust that the nation should suffer for the sin of one man; but a great many points have to be considered before coming to a decision. The spirit of theft that broke out in Achan may have been

latent among the people, and so the defeat would be a discipline to cure them of that state of heart.

This age is not an age of trust; that is a lesson we have got to learn—confidence in the justice of God. There is a Jewish legend to this effect. Moses, it is said, once complained, as a great many others have since done, of the apparent injustice in the world; he had a vision, and in the vision he saw a watering-place in the oasis. A soldier stayed to drink, and departing dropped a purse of gold; a small boy passed by, and finding the purse, went off with it; next an old man stopped to rest; while he was there the soldier, having missed his purse, returned, and because the old man could not produce the gold when required killed him! "How unjust," exclaimed the impatient Moses. "Not at all," replied the Almighty, "That old man was a murderer, and had murdered the father of the small boy."

4. All our deeds, whether for good or evil, have some effect, however unappreciable, upon the life of the nation. The figure of the body is an apt illustration, when one member is sick the body is not in perfect health. It is the same with the body politic.

5. The sin of Achan was disobedience, theft, sacrilege; did he repent of it? Probably. He made a true and complete confession of his sin—of his deed and its motive. Next, there is a very comforting passage in Hosea ii. 15 that bears upon the subject.

The Valley of Achor, where Achan troubled Israel, is called a "door of hope." The dark side of the picture is terribly dark—the theft, the deceit, the punishment, but Hosea hints at the brighter side, as if Achan had died penitent, as if his "I have sinned" had been accepted, and he had passed away with the hope of salvation.

6. Here is also an instance of a blessing in disguise. "My son," said Joshua to Achan, most tenderly, when dealing with the case, "Give, I pray thee, glory to the God of Israel." For what? we ask in surprise. Surely it was for having discovered the sin, as the shortest road to repentance. However much we may dread being found out it should be a good thing for us. The more serious the sin, the greater the fear which begins to weigh upon our life; confession lifts that burden, and we are able to thank God with a light heart.

CHAPTER II., Sec. 4.

Wednesday.

THE REPENTANCE OF DAVID.

2 Sam. XII. 1 to 26.

Notes :—

1. Having taken the first wrong step, it is easier to take the second; nay, it often almost seems as if we were obliged to take the second. A boy running downhill, who can't stop till he gets to the bottom, is a very apt illustration of a man who begins to go wrong. The path of sin is a steep downhill path. One wrong deed leads to another, as we see again and again in the Bible, and as we must know from our own experience. We need not dwell upon the ugly story of David's adultery with Bathsheba, and his subsequent murder of Uriah, the husband, to hide his crime. To see how true it is to life, we have only to compare it with the stories recorded in the modern newspapers. But now we turn over the leaf to read the beautiful account of the repentance.

2. Nathan's parable of the ewe lamb is exquisite.

We have often a very accurate judgment in estimating the sins and faults of other people, whilst singularly blind as to our own. This might be turned to account. Being a good judge of character should help us in our spiritual life.

3. David, without hesitation, passed a sentence of death, but when Nathan came to apply it, David's decision was set aside. The same punishment is not meted out to the same offence under all circumstances, even in human courts of justice, much less in Divine. This compassionate consideration for others should guide us in our dealings with those in fault. We must never forget that while the sin must be dealt with severely, the sinner must be treated tenderly.

4. "Thou art the man!" What a thunderbolt! What an unexpected revelation! All at once, after a year of darkness, David saw his conduct in its true light. The story is told with consummate skill. These simple, straightforward words of condemnation stand out for all time. Whenever we wake up to the consciousness of having done wrong we hear them whispered in our heart. Our colloquial expression, "the cap fits," is another way of saying the same thing, "Thou art the man!"

5. When Nathan had done speaking, David replied, frankly and humbly, "I have sinned." It was a genuine confession; therefore Nathan immediately rejoined, "The Lord also hath put away thy

sin." David must indeed have been comforted by that unreserved absolution. This is one of the great benefits of Confession nowadays—the assurance of forgiveness.

6. Truly God brings good out of evil; and from this incident we have inherited two rich blessings—(*a*) That wonderful outpouring of a penitent heart, the 51st Psalm. (*b*) That bright and early intimation of a future life, " I shall go to him, but he shall not return to me."

7. By far the most important question raised by the life of David, and by the history of this sin in particular, is—How can a man who is capable of committing such foul sins be called a man after God's heart? It is a question that has troubled many Christians, and that is made the most of by unbelievers. The answer is not far to seek, though it is missed by so many. Those who know and *love* the Psalms will have discovered the secret for themselves. God judges by character. It often happens that a man of really fine and noble character does some deed of great enormity that damns him with the world. We must always remember that the world condemned Christ and Socrates. We must never forget that the man who is capable of the highest things is also capable of the lowest. Mountain climbing is very dangerous, we may easily fall down a precipice. Our future state does not depend on two or three deeds conspicuously bad, but on our

career as a whole. Only God's eye can view a life, man's is often obstructed by a single flaw.

> "The sin that practice burns into the blood,
> And not the one dark hour which brings remorse,
> Will brand us after."
> —*Tennyson*, "*Merlin and Vivien.*"

CHAPTER II., Sec. 5.

Thursday.

THE REPENTANCE OF S. PETER.
Luke xxii. 54 to 63.

Notes :—

1. The threefold denial of S. Peter, both in its prediction and in its accomplishment, is given by all four Evangelists, with a variety of detail that proves they are independent writers, but does not show they contradict themselves. The accounts are as follow :—

First denial. All say the question was put by a damsel, whom S. John tells us was the portress.

Second denial. S. Matthew says, "another woman"; S. Mark, "the same damsel"; S. Luke, "another man"; S. John, "they say." The last is the key to unlock the problem. There is a great crowd round the fire, the portress tells her suspicions, several people repeat the accusation.

Third denial. This explanation is further brought out in the narratives of this third denial. S. Luke says, "another"; S. John, "a kinsman of Malchus";

SS. Matthew and Mark, "they that stood by." So these differences are not a defect, but an ornament. Taken together they reproduce the life of a crowd, and vouch for the truth of the writers of the Gospels, who dared to throw down such apparent contradictions. Let anyone who doubts this, watch a crowd at work, and he will soon be convinced that it is true.

2. The whole story is an example of the proverb, "Pride goes before a fall." Boasting is particularly offensive, especially in the more sacred relationships of life. It is always bad taste, and often untrue. In the case of S. Peter, it is very distressing when we remember he was one of the three favoured disciples. It was an independent spirit, such an independent spirit as is characteristic of the nineteenth century, and forms a hideous ideal, which repels more than attracts. Each man for himself, is the principle of selfishness, in contrast with all men for each other, which is the principle of love. We are taught to believe in the Communion of Saints.

3. In the case of David we saw how one sin involved another. Here is a second example in the threefold denial—linked lies. The cursing and swearing on the last occasion is only mentioned by S. Mark, who is supposed to have written at the dictation of S. Peter. Others threw a veil over a feature not essential to their narrative. He himself confessed all. We should not delight in the short-

comings of other folks; we should not shrink from revealing our own in Confession.

4. "The Lord turned and looked upon Peter." What a searching instrument of conversion!—the eye of his Friend, and such a Friend. This sentence is one of those that stick in the mind, of which there are so many in the Bible, both proving its cleverness, and affording us a definite subject of meditation easily remembered. One flash of the eye, one penetrating glance, and S. Peter was recalled to himself, a changed man. There was rebuke, tenderness, and grief. The eye of God is not meant to be alarming. "Thou, God, seest me," was Hagar's prayer of implicit trust, and should never be used as a bogey text with which to frighten children.

5. The repentance was complete. It is very graphically described. When he thought thereon he flung his mantle over his head (ἐπιβαλὼν, Mark xiv. 72) and wept bitterly—wept aloud, continued weeping. Such tears are acceptable.

6. At the Sea of Tiberias we have an allusion to the threefold denial in the threefold affirmation (see John xxi. 15-18). Thrice our Lord asked, "Lovest thou Me?" and at the third time S. Peter was grieved, not only at the hint backwards to the denial, but at the form of the question itself, which is lost in the English version. In Greek there are two words for love, a higher word and a lower. S. Peter always uses the last; twice our Lord uses

the first, but the third time He uses S. Peter's own word, and seems to question even his lower standard of love. No wonder S. Peter was grieved. This narrative exemplifies the third commandment, which teaches that because our words belong to God we must be careful of them.

CHAPTER II., Sec. 6.

𝔉riday.

THE REPENTANCE OF THE DYING THIEF.

Luke xxiii. 39 to 44.

Notes :—

1. Both the robbers reproached Christ; one railed on Him with abusive and insulting language, but the other rebuked his companion, and bore valuable testimony to our Lord's innocence—" This man hath done nothing amiss."

2. No blessing comes without faith, and the thief before he secured the one, showed the other in a remarkable degree. "Lord!" he exclaimed, "remember me when Thou comest into Thy Kingdom." He probably did not understand the full meaning of his own words, but having heard our Lord teaching about the Kingdom, he now felt convinced of the absolute sincerity of the speaker.

3. He required a very severe punishment to awaken him to a sense of his own guilt. That is the chief use of punishment, and happy is the man who repents before he experiences the torment of hell.

From this story we learn that repentance is possible at the eleventh hour, as we say; but from our experience of life we learn that it is very rare. As a man lives, so he dies. If his strength of mind is fairly well maintained to the end, the opinions of a lifetime are maintained also; if he is exceedingly weak, he begins to cry on the Almighty, about Whom he learnt at school, but has forgotten ever since. This sort of thing is no good; it is even contemptible. "Not every one that saith unto Me, Lord! Lord! shall enter into the Kingdom of Heaven, but he that doeth the will of My Father." It is a true proverb—

> "The devil was ill; the devil a monk would be:
> The devil got well; then devil a monk was he."

It often happens that when folks are dangerously ill they make professions of repentance, which are never realized on their recovery. Any priest could supply plenty of examples. I knew an old gentleman who was in the habit of drinking, and after every serious bout was taken ill; then he sent for the priest to make his confession, but as soon as he was well again he drank as before, till he died.

A short time ago a woman lay dying in one of the great London hospitals. She suffered from a horribly painful disease, and the doctors told her it would be necessary to put her under the influence of anæsthetics and to send her to sleep. They asked her whether, before they did so, she would like to see the Chaplain. Her reply was awful in its sad truth. "No!" she said; "I've lived without God, and I must die without Him."

4. Repentance, we cannot be too often reminded, consists of three parts, contrition, *i.e.*, sorrow, confession, and amendment. This is why, in the Absolution at Matins and Evensong, we are exhorted to pray for repentance after having confessed, for the third part is still to follow, and for that we pray. In the case of the dying thief there were only a few hours for amendment, but he made the best use of them; having begun with reproaches, impenitent until the last opportunity, he ended with prayer, and faith, and rebukes to his companion in sin, which became a testimony to the multitude. We may believe that many murderers die penitent, the trial and condemnation having made the crisis in their lives; but we have every reason to doubt the genuineness of the repentance of those who go on still in their wickedness, up to the closing scenes of life, and who die in the ordinary course of nature, without any startling event to wake them to a sense of their perilous condition.

5. Contrition may be of two sorts, that differ in degree, but not in kind: perfect and imperfect. The latter is called attrition; it is sorrow for sin when the motive is good, but not very high. If a man is sorry because God is grieved, that is contrition;

but if he be only sorry because he runs the risk of losing eternal life, that is attrition : the second motive is good, but not so worthy as the other. It must be confessed that a great number of penitents never get beyond attrition. The teaching and discipline of the Salvation Army in this respect is admirable. The practice of the Church has become very lax, and requires bracing.

CHAPTER II., Sec. 7.

Saturday.

THE REPENTANCE OF A CORINTHIAN.

1 Cor. v. 1 to 7 and 2 Cor. ii. 1 to 12.

Notes :—

1. The name of this fast young Greek is not given, and the hideous story is only set down in the briefest outline for the sake of the principles involved. A man had pretended to marry his step-mother! Public opinion was not shocked! Why should he not do so? She was no relation of his! argued the men of the world at Corinth in the first century, as they are arguing in the nineteenth to-day. Immediately S. Paul heard of it he excommunicated the offender. So much for the first passage.

2. Six months passed away. In the meantime the sinner repented, and repudiated the incestuous connection with his father's widow. S. Paul heard of the genuineness of his sorrow, and sent word to say that he must be absolved. On the first occasion he was sharply stern, on the second sensitively tender. The punishment, having produced the effect

which was intended, must be removed at once, lest it should prove greater than the man could bear, and drive him to go on in his evil courses. That would defeat the object in view, that would give Satan the advantage over them (v. 11). Therefore the penitent, being sorry and having confessed, must be helped to amendment by being restored to Communion. Such is the conclusion of the story contained in the second passage.

3. The first great principle is the power of absolution possessed by the Church. The history of that power is as follows. Christ declared at Capernaum "The Son of Man hath power ($\dot{\epsilon}\xi o \upsilon \sigma i a \nu$) on earth to forgive sins." The word used for power means delegated authority. As Son of God He possessed it by right; as Son of Man He received it from the Father. The full force of the expression, "The Son of Man hath power on earth to forgive sins," was caught by the multitude when they thanked God, Who "had given such power unto men." The power possessed by the Representative Man henceforth belonged to the race, and is as much required now as then. It was a power that could be passed to others; so on one solemn occasion our Lord breathed on the twelve, and said, "Whosoever sins ye forgive they are forgiven, and whosoever sins ye retain they are retained" (See John xx. 23, R.V.). A little later we find that the power had been passed on to S. Paul, who exercised it in a curious way in the case before

us, for though absent, he was consulted, and said that he excommunicated, and that he forgave, while the sentences of condemnation and acquittal were actually pronounced by someone else, either the messenger who carried his letter, or some local priest. Finally, amongst ourselves we still find the power, for whenever a priest is ordained the bishop gives him the same commission that Christ gave His Apostles, using the same words (see Ordinal). And a direct form of absolution is provided in the Office for the Visitation of the Sick.

4. The explanation is simple. To God only it appertaineth to forgive sins; He is the source of the power, and He confirms the sentence. It is with Him the sinner has to be reconciled, and He alone knows whether the reconciliation has taken place. Man pronounces sentence, as in a court of law, but sentence of condemnation does not make an innocent man guilty, nor does a sentence of acquittal make a guilty man innocent; it is the same in the Confessional. The priest forgives sins in the same sense as God does, though God alone knows the result. Neither the priest nor God (we write in all reverence) can forgive sins in an absolute sense; it would be a contradiction; God could not forgive an impenitent man; the sentence depends on the sinner.

5. We must not fail to observe the effect of excommunication. The man was reduced to exceeding grief by the loss of his Church privileges. Now

in these days of decayed discipline is this the case? The contrast is a very sad one. Few value these privileges at their true worth. If a man is suspended at Church he feels no loss, but goes to the Dissenters, who give him everything he wants—stones for bread! and even serpents for eggs, which sting him to death.

6. The second great principle involved is faithfulness to the marriage laws. In these days of the failure of marriage, the laws do not require to be relaxed, but made more stringent. Men must not be allowed to marry their deceased wife's sister, nor must divorced persons, whether innocent or guilty, be allowed to re-marry.

CHAPTER III., Sec. 1.

Second Sunday.

THE MEDITATION OF ELIJAH.

1 KINGS XIX. 1 to 19.

NOTES :—

1. After the grand scene of the sacrifice and slaughter of the false prophets on Mount Carmel, Elijah fled for his life to Beersheba, in the Kingdom of Judah; and there, retiring into the wilderness, he was miraculously fed with bread and water, and sent on to Mount Horeb, where he remained in the strength of that meat forty days and forty nights, meditating upon the problems of life.

2. In the hurry and bustle of modern civilization not nearly enough time is given to meditation, hence ill-digested thoughts, ill-considered deeds, and hasty actions are so common; hence impatience, irritability, and temper are so rampant. We are even in too great a hurry to be polite to one another. The calm of the cloister is unknown in the nineteenth century. Thus there is so much friction in life, and so little ease. It is a thousand pities that every Church in

the country is not open all day long for the weary and heavy-laden to creep into, for a few moments of repose and refreshment. Throw open one Church, and the success will not be very apparent, for two reasons; first, because men have forgotten under long Protestant rule the true use of a Church, and, secondly, because few will know that it is open if the majority are closed. Throw open all the Churches, and the result, we feel sure, will be startling; people will flock to them as to havens of rest in a troubled land. Hence we should see the immense value of such seasons as Lent, recurring periodically every year, to encourage meditation. We are reminded, by a beautiful hymn on the Passion, of the work of a few moments of contemplation of our Lord on the Cross—

> "Sweet the moments rich in blessing,
> Which before the Cross I spend.
> Life and health and peace possessing
> From the sinner's dying Friend."

How few ever sing this verse sincerely! How few ever succeed in feeling the words! The world would be the better if they did. Every one should have a Crucifix in the house. It is within the reach of all, as a beautiful one, made to hang up, can be bought for the small sum of fourpence. Most families have two rooms, in one of which the members might take it in turn to kneel before the Crucifix; other things have to be done in rotation, then why not this? The poorest can be religious. Few have the excuse of only one room, and those can go to the Churches, as can, of course, the rest. Every Church should have a Calvary, a huge figure of Christ upon the Cross, to excite the devotion of the faithful, and to it streams of worshippers would come to pray.

3. Elijah sitting under the juniper tree was very near suicide. He had to be taught the exceeding great value of life. He had to be encouraged, for he was despairing; and he came from his retreat a wiser, and a better man, calm, strong, brave.

4. The weirdly grand manifestations on Horeb appeal to our imagination. The lesson of the still, small voice is the same as that of our Lord's Parable, "The seed growing secretly" (Mark iv. 26-30). "The Kingdom of God cometh not with observation" (Luke xvii. 20). Although unknown to Elijah, the true religion had not been stamped out by the idolatries of the Court, but was maintained quietly, for there were 7,000, perhaps 7,000 families, who had never bowed the knee to Baal. We should not be discouraged at the irreligion of the world, we should rather make the most of the good folk, as a means of spreading the faith. A little leaven leaveneth the whole lump. A small band of faithful will soon attract adherents. A cluster of violets in the hedgerow spreads perfume on the air. The influence of one single consistent life is incalculable.

In the case of the 7,000, the reformation that they wrought in their country in the twelve short years of the reign of Jehoram, son of Ahab, was wonderful, for when Jehu conspired against him, and determined to put down the worship of Baal, all his worshippers, without a single exception, were able to assemble within the four walls of his house, so there could not have been very many who were ready to own him as God.

CHAPTER III., Sec. 2.

Monday.

THE MEDITATION OF ISAAC.
Gen. xxiv. 61 to end.

Notes :—

1. It was time for Isaac to marry; he had lost his mother, and required a wife. He lived a long way from his own country, yet wished for a woman of his own tribe. He did not go to seek one for himself, as we should have done, but sent an old and trusted steward, Eliezer of Damascus (xv. 2), to find one for him. This servant, skilled in affairs of the heart, was eminently successful on his mission, and brought back Rebekah, the young man's first cousin. When they returned to Palestine, and were nearing home, it was eventide, and they found Isaac meditating in the fields. The girl turned out all that could be desired, and Isaac "loved" her.

2. No doubt a personal choice of a wife is far better than having a third person to negotiate the marriage. No doubt a long study of character is preferable to the young people meeting for the first

(e) "*Soberly.*" If the last rule was positive, this rule may perhaps be stated negatively. Do it advisedly; don't let passion decide the matter in a hurry. Keep self-controlled; don't be like a drunken man, who does not quite know what he is doing.

No one need begin to ask if marriage is a failure until the conditions of success have been tried. Those cases where there has been no attempt to keep the rules do not count. Marriage has not failed, but man.

CHAPTER III., SEC. 3.

Tuesday.

THE MEDITATION OF SAMUEL.

1 SAM. III.

NOTES :—

1. Everyone must be familiar with Sant's beautiful attempt to portray the child Samuel kneeling up in bed to listen to the Divine Voice. Though the boy is not altogether satisfactory in point of age, being too young, the picture is an attractive one, especially to a child; and when a small boy I remember being lifted up every night at bedtime to kiss the boy in the picture. It was a remarkable revival of an old Catholic practice in a family that was by no means noted for advanced Churchmanship. People nowadays often kiss portraits of their sweetheart, but rarely objects of religious devotion. Yet I once had the privilege of seeing a rough East End boy receive a Crucifix from his friend, at the close of the Three Hours' Service on Good Friday, and kiss it before leaving the Church.

2. In the Catechism our names are recited, not only to recall our Baptism, but also sometimes for the sake of the meaning of the name. Shakespeare asks, "What's in a name?" Often a good deal. Samuel means "asked of God." He was welcomed to the home of a childless wife. We are afraid that the newcomer is not always very gladly received in a large family, which is more of a disgrace than an honour. Samuel also may mean "heard of God," which has a double application; the mother was heard; her earnest prayers for a son were granted; also the boy himself was heard, and became a famous prophet.

3. "The child Samuel ministered." Then, as now, all ages were pressed into the service of God. "Heaven is near us in our infancy," writes Wordsworth. A boy has the high privilege of standing at the Altar by the priest at the very moment of Consecration. Again, I must refer to an East End boy of 16, who bows so reverently in the Presence of the Blessed Sacrament, that his very action is a lesson in reverence to the whole congregation—or to those who have eyes to see.

4. "Here am I!" What smart readiness! What instant obedience! What anxiousness to please! What reverence from youth to age! What unselfish consideration for his old guardian!

5. "Samuel did not yet know the Lord." This is the explanation given for his not recognizing

the voice. He was virtuous, but had never heard such a voice before. The boy's goodness is unmistakable, and is revealed in every line of the narrative.

6. "Speak, for Thy servant heareth!" LORD is omitted, not from lack, but excess of reverence. The name used is Jehovah. As we shrink from using the name "Jesus" in ordinary conversation, so the Jews shrank from using the great name of God, generally substituting some less awful title. It might be all very well for an old man like Eli to use the great name, Samuel would think, but for a small boy like himself to do so would be presumptuous.

7. "Samuel lay until the morning," in bed, but not asleep, meditating. He had much to occupy his thoughts—the vision, the call, the impending calamity, his own future career, and the destiny of the nation, etc. Bed is often a place for serious meditation, and the opportunities should not be missed. Sleeplessness can be used, and its irritability calmed, by having some holy thought to turn over in the mind. When we enter our room at night we should leave the world behind. The test of our success is how we wake in the morning. Is life full of anxieties? How do we rise to meet them? Refreshed or worried? In the first case religion has triumphed, in the latter the world. Next, on a sick bed we have much to think about. We have to

review the past and plan for the future. We have to sound our faith, so as to be able to answer the priest when he asks us if we believe. We have to sum up our sins, that we may be ready when he invites us to confess (See Office for Visitation of Sick).

CHAPTER III., Sec. 4.

Wednesday.

THE MEDITATION OF ASAPH.
Psalm LXXVII.

NOTES:—

1. Asaph was one of those placed by David over the service of song, rendered first in the Tabernacle, and afterwards in the Temple (1 Chron. vi. 31, 39). We may call him a director of the choir. And since he became so famous, we may regard him as head or master of the choir. In performing his office he adorned it. In the days of Hezekiah he was regarded as a seer, and counted second only to David (2 Chron. xxix. 30). The music was instrumental as well as vocal. There were harps, psalteries, cymbals, etc., upon which the performers were said to *prophesy* (1 Chron. xxv. 1), so important was their work in setting *forth* the praise of God. They must have been very numerous, for at the return from Captivity, when the Temple worship, no doubt, was not rendered on a scale so magnificent as formerly, the number of choristers alone was 128 (Ezra ii. 41).

Asaph evidently founded a school of poets, who were known as the Sons of Asaph, and who wrote many of the Psalms which bear his name. It is not any of the Psalms in particular that we shall consider, but shall make a few remarks on the Psalter as a whole.

2. The Psalms are by various known and unknown authors, whose lives covered a period of some 500 years. They are divided, but not chronologically, into five books, and each book ends with a doxology. Book I., Psalms i. to xli.; Book II., Psalms xlii. to lxxii.; Book III., Psalms lxxiii. to lxxxix.; Book IV., Psalms xc. to cvi.; Book V., Psalms cvii. to cl.

3. The use of Psalms in Christian worship is referred to four times in the New Testament (1 Cor. xiv. 26; Eph. v. 19; Col. iii. 16, and James v. 13). With us the Psalter is recited publicly once a month: and the Gregorian tones seem admirably adapted for such recitation. The custom of men and boys chanting alternate verses accounts for the other custom of men and women sitting on different sides of the Church, in order that they might "speak to one another in psalms" (Eph. v. 19). There is no need to stand while the Psalms are sung, as they are by no means entirely hymns of praise.

4. The selection of special Psalms is perhaps referred to once in the New Testament. After the institution

of the Mass, Jesus and His Apostles "sung a hymn" (Matt. xxvi. 30), which was most likely the great Hallel (Psalms cxiii. to cxviii.), sung at all Jewish festivals. In our Prayer Book special Psalms are provided for the four great Feasts and the two great Fasts, but special Psalms for many other occasions are coming into general use according to the fashion of the Middle Ages. There are also special Psalms for weddings, churchings, funerals, etc. Then the introits too, sung while the Ministers are entering the sanctuary and preparing to say Mass, are mostly taken from the Psalter.

5. The chief characteristic of Hebrew poetry is parallelism, in which ideas run side by side. It may be said to be of three kinds :—

(*a*) Ideas of similitude.
> "The heavens declare the glory of God;
> And the firmament sheweth His handiwork" (xix. 1).

(*b*) Ideas of contrast.
> "There is neither speech nor language:
> But their voices are heard among them"
> —(xix. 3).

(*c*) Ideas of sequence.
> "The Lord is my Shepherd:
> Therefore can I lack nothing" (xxiii. 1).

The stirring device of the chorus is not forgotten; the most remarkable example of which is in Psalm cvii. 8, 15, 21, 31. "O that men would therefore praise the Lord for His goodness: and declare the wonders that He doeth for the children of men."

Dialogue is often introduced, *e.g.*, in the well-known Venite, Psalm xcv., when the author speaks in verses 1 to 9, and the Almighty from verse 9 to end. The glorious Ascension Psalm, No. xxiv., is clearly dramatic, questions, and answers, and choruses being taken up by different parts of the choir.

6. The Psalter is a rich treasury of devotion for all sorts and conditions of men. Each one must discover its beauties and its appropriateness for himself. But as a set of suggestions it may be shown how it illustrates the Mass.

(*a*) The sacrifice of praise and thanksgiving.
    "Let us come before His Presence with thanksgiving" (xcv. 2).

(*b*) A splendid ritual.
    "O worship the Lord in the beauty of holiness" (xcvi. 9).

(*c*) Approach to the Altar.
    "Then will I go unto the Altar of God" (xliii. 4, A.V.).

(*d*) Lavabo: the priest washing his hands.
    "I will wash my hands in innocency, O Lord" (xxvi. 6).

(*e*) Sursum Corda.
    "Lift up your hands in the Sanctuary" (cxxxiv. 3).

(*f*) Benedictus.
   " Blessed is He that cometh in the name of the Lord " (cxviii. 26).
(*g*) Real Presence.
   " The Lord is in His holy temple " (xi. 4).
(*h*) Communion.
   "I will receive the cup of salvation " (cxvi. 12).

CHAPTER III., Sec. 5.

Thursday.

THE MEDITATION OF HEZEKIAH.

2 Kings xix. 6 to end.

Notes :—

1. Sennacherib, King of Assyria, after his imperious manner, sent a letter to Hezekiah, saying, that it was useless for him to trust in God, that the other gods had not delivered the other nations, neither would his God deliver him, so he might as well open his gates without further delay. Immediately Hezekiah received this insulting letter he took it to the Temple, and, actually spreading it before the Lord, prayed for help and deliverance.

2. Hezekiah was a religious man, who had his life prolonged for his personal goodness, and, we may say, had his reign prolonged for the fairly satisfactory state of his people. Louis XIV. said, "Je suis d'état." Hezekiah could have said the same in a far truer and nobler sense. He spoke on behalf of the State. The Church was co-extensive with the State, and was, as we should say, established.

When the king did as he chose, the effect on the State was disastrous, both morally and politically. Here we are taught as plainly as possible that religion must be established, must be recognized by the State : the State must be religious. Let those folks, who are clamouring for Disestablishment in England, pause to consider the terrible result and the far-reaching consequences of the change. The State would be purely secular. There would be no religious functions whatever in connection with any State affair. Religion would be entirely ignored, the monarch would be no longer its defender. The marks of Christianity would have to be erased wherever found. There would be no official recognition of Christ. We have already experienced the disastrous consequences of education without religion, and should not wish to make the experiment of government without it. Any man of common sense can estimate the character of Disestablishment by the company it keeps with Disendowment, *i.e.*, with robbery, which is also sacrilege.

3. The Church, in her wisdom, does not ignore the mental means of grace, she only puts them in a far lower position than the sacramental. They are themselves of great value. We get real good from the Bible and other books of devotion ; we are strengthened and fortified by communing with God in the quiet hours of meditation. Hezekiah knew the value of this, and set us the example when he

took the letter to the Temple. As children take their troubles to their protectors, so men should take theirs to the Almighty. It is wonderfully comforting, wonderfully sustaining.

4. Hezekiah received a letter, and went to pray. When we receive a black-edged letter, containing bad news, who can tell the effect of an upward word of prayer, before opening the letter, to help us receive the news with equanimity. Such little habits of prayer at all times give us marvellous courage, and bring God so near and so dear. They afford the best means of acquiring that most invaluable quality, presence of mind; they cultivate the power in us of doing and saying the right thing at the right moment. This constant recognition of God is of the very essence of true religion. God orders all the affairs of the universe; we should learn to see this. Do we receive a benefit? Let there be an immediate word of thanks. Do we fear an evil? May it be averted. Do we experience a misfortune? May we bear it with resignation. Are we setting out on a journey? Let us ask for protection. Are we getting up? Let us rejoice at the beginning of another day. Are we going to bed? Let us commend ourselves to God's safe keeping. Religion consists, not in pulling a long face, not in asking other people if they are saved, not in rebuking our neighbour, but in the personal attitude of the soul to God, and the influence we exercise at all times.

The Meditation of Hezekiah.

5. Compare with this the glorious Psalm xci. It is of unknown date and authorship, but would have made a splendid pæan of thanksgiving after the deliverance from the Assyrians. Notice especially the following points, which suit the case of Hezekiah:

(a) The absolute trust in God (v. 2).

(b) The pestilence that carried off the enemies of God (v. 7).

(c) The protection that kept the pestilence at a distance (v. 7).

(d) The love that is not disappointed (v. 14).

(e) The extension of life (v. 16).

CHAPTER III., Sec. 6.

Friday.

THE MEDITATION OF CHRIST.
Luke vi. 12.

NOTES:—

1. A mountain is a wonderful and inspiring feature of nature. It suggests firmness, eternity, difficulty to be overcome, aspiration by its lofty peak, meditation in its solitude, and, when covered with snow, purity. It is fitted to be a sanctuary. The tendency to take possession of the hills in the name of the Lord is a true and right one. When in the Old Testament we read that the high places were removed, it was not the position that was objected to, but the falseness of the worship. In England the Cathedrals of Durham and Lincoln are magnificently placed. In France the heights above Paris, Lyons, and Marseilles are crowned with fine Churches.

2. In the Bible, what events took place on hills? This is not such a useless question as it may appear, for our ability to answer shows a general knowledge of the contents of the Holy Book.

The Meditation of Christ. 63

(1) The Ark rested on Mount Ararat.
(2) Isaac was offered on Mount Gerizim in the land of Moriah, *i.e.*, of vision.
(3) The Law was given on Mount Sinai.
(4) Aaron died on Mount Hor.
(5) Moses was buried by God on Mount Nebo.
(6) Saul and Jonathan were slain on Mount Gilboa.
(7) The Temple was built on Mount Moriah.
(8) Elijah contended on Mount Carmel with the prophets of Baal.
(9) The Mount of Olives was a favourite retreat of our Lord.
(10) Mount Hermon witnessed His Transfiguration.
(11) Mount Calvary was the scene of His death.

3. Christ continued all night in prayer. This fact astonishes us in two particulars, the immense difficulty of the exercise, and the necessity for it in the case of our Lord. This astonishment is not altogether to our credit; the first thought shows slackness in practice, and the second defect of Ideal. In the case of our Lord it was an infinite delight, a necessity of His nature. In our case it is hard of attainment. Of old the warriors watched from eve till morn in prayer before the Altar, previous to their knighthood. We nowadays suffer from want of serious thought. The contemplative side of life has been much neglected since the downfall of the Monasteries.

4. There were many times and seasons of prayer

in the life of our Lord, and the Gospel of S. Luke may almost be called the Gospel of prayer, because he alone records many of the instances, which are marked below with a P.

(1) At Baptism (Luke iii. 21). P.
(2) The day after S. Peter's mother-in-law was healed. "A great while before day." "In a desert place" (Mark i. 35; Luke iv. 42).
(3) After healing a leper. "In the deserts" (Luke v. 16). P.
(4) Before choosing the Apostles. "All night" (Luke vi. 12). P.
(5) When feeding the five thousand. "Looking up to Heaven He blessed" (Luke ix. 16).
(6) After the five thousand were fed. "On a mountain" all night, for He came upon the Apostles in the boat, in the fourth or last watch of the night (Matt. xiv. 23, 25).
(7) When feeding the four thousand He gave thanks (Matt. xv. 36).
(8) Before S. Peter's great confession. Intercession (Luke ix. 18). P.
(9) On the Mount of Transfiguration (Luke ix. 28, 29). P.
(10) After the return of the seventy (Luke x. 21).
(11) At the raising of Lazarus (John xi. 41.) P.
(12) When the deputation of Greeks arrived (John xii. 28). P.

The Meditation of Christ.

(13) Over the first cup. Thanksgiving (Luke xxii. 17). P.
(14) At the institution of the Eucharist—over the bread (Luke xxii. 19).
(15) At the institution of the Eucharist—over the cup (Luke xxii. 20).
(16) For S. Peter (Luke xxii. 32). P.
(17) The Prayer of the great High Priest (John xvii.). P.
(18) In the garden (Matt. xxvi. 39, 42, 44; see also Luke xxii. 41-45).
(19) For His murderers (Luke xxiii. 34). P.
(20) At the hour of darkness (Matt. xxvii. 46). Not mentioned by S. Luke.
(21) At the moment of death (Luke xxiii. 46). P.

All these Prayers will repay study. In Nos. 10, 11, 17, 18, 19, 20, 21, the words are given. In Nos. 1, 2, 3, 4, 6, 8, 9, only the fact is recorded. S. Luke records all the instances except Nos. 6, 7, 11, 12, 17, 20, and has nine peculiar (P.) to himself.

5. "Prayer is the contemplation of the facts of life from the highest point of view." "It is the soliloquy of a beholding and jubilant soul" (*Emerson,* Essays ii. 1).

CHAPTER III., SEC. 7.

Saturday.

THE MEDITATION OF TIMOTHY.

1 TIM. IV.

NOTES:—

1. This is a short but suggestive chapter. The reason of its selection for this series is to be found in the command of verse 15, "Meditate on these things." It is in order to secure the exact word that this chapter has been chosen rather than, say, chapters i. or iii. of the Second Epistle, which will be especially referred to in the last note.

2. "In the latter times some shall depart from the Faith" (v. 1), *i.e.*, all Dissenters and Apostates. "If thou put the brethren in remembrance of these things, thou shalt be a good minister of Jesus Christ." The first quotation is an exact prophecy of what is being fulfilled in our own days, and therefore opens up a question of modern life; *i.e.*, the relation of Churchmen to Dissenters. The second quotation instructs the clergy in their duty of pointing out to the laity the bearings of the situation.

It is most important, in these days of inexact thought, to teach precisely the difference between right and wrong views of truth. The barest statement only is possible here. A thoughtful mind will perceive at once that Church and Dissent cannot both be right upon those points about which they differ. Further, as many of these points are vital, it is a matter of very great importance whether we attend Church or the Meeting House. It is not only wicked to say, " It does not much matter," and " All mean the same thing in the end," it is positively foolish, and shows that the speaker is entirely ignorant of what he is talking. As such ignorance is very common, the expression is very dangerous. S. Paul tells the young bishop, his disciple, that it is his duty to speak very clearly to his people on the subject, and that his own qualification for office actually depends on the perspicuity of his teaching. Hundreds of the modern clergy speak very timidly on the matter, if they speak at all; some even say in plain words, " It doesn't matter." They should teach the people in clear, straightforward language, that Dissenters have erred from the Faith; that dissent or schism is a very bad sin, judging from the company it keeps in the Litany, with sedition, conspiracy, rebellion, hardness of heart, and contempt of God's Word and Commandment; and that it is a sin on the part of Churchmen to assist Dissenters in any way, by attending their Chapels or giving them money. Thus only, according to the standard of S. Paul, can each one qualify as "a good minister of Jesus Christ."

3. "Bodily exercise profiteth a little." The "a" is important. S. Paul does not mean to cast a slur on exercise: it is very good: in its proper place it is excellent; but it is not everything. Man has a spirit as well as a body, and only half his nature is developed if he pays attention exclusively to his body, to the utter neglect of his soul. Yet this is what all those folks do who try to banish religion from life.

4. The 14th is the sacramental verse. The sacrament of orders is alluded to: the outward and visible sign being the bishop's hands; the inward and spiritual grace, *i.e.*, the gift, the authority to dispense the rest of the sacraments. Ordination by a bishop, called Apostolic Succession, is indispensable; without it the Church would be destroyed. Dissenters, having lost it, are outside the Divine Society, except so far as they have been baptized. They may be regenerate; they cannot be renewed.

5. "Give attendance to reading," *i.e.*, to study. Everyone should read at least the Bible, and some other book of devotion. The man who *knows* his Bible, even if he reads no other book, would be well educated. From a secular point of view alone it contains every sort of literature—history, philosophy, ethics, poetry, etc., by the best authors. From a religious point of view it is an inexhaustible treasury,

providing spiritual exercises for all sorts and conditions of men, in every age, in every country. It is sadly neglected nowadays. People do not know their Bibles as well as they did a generation ago, to their own infinite loss. The object of this little book is to encourage the study of Scripture, which, we hope, will be revived. In 2 Tim. i. 5 and iii. 15 we have exquisite peeps into the boyhood of Timothy. They are attractive fragments of personal biography, very precious. If nothing is known of S. Paul's two letters, these few verses are sure to be familiar. Once heard, they catch in the memory, because they are interesting. We are introduced into the home circle and the family life; we see the little fellow being trained at his mother's knee in knowledge of the Scriptures. He is held up for our example until the word of God becomes "a lantern unto our feet, and a light unto our paths" (Psalm cxix. 105).

CHAPTER IV., Sec. 1.

Third Sunday.

THE INVESTIGATION OF THE SPIES.

Num. xiii. 17 to end, and xiv. 34.

Notes:—

1. This expedition of the spies was most wisely ordered. It was necessary that the Israelites should have some practical knowledge of the country and the peoples they were going to fight against. We live under the same necessity. In the spiritual combat we fight with enemies who are trying to keep us from the Promised Land. We fight with vice for the possession of virtue. Hence we study sins as well as graces. We study graces that we may value them; we may study sins that we may estimate their power. An old woman is as harmless as a dove; a man of the world is as wise as a serpent. A Christian must avoid both these characters; he must combine a knowledge of good and evil.

2. There were twelve spies sent to search—to investigate. In this word search we get the keynote for the week. May we do our work as thoroughly

as the spies did theirs. They penetrated as far as Rehob, a place in the extreme north of the country, in the valley of Lebanon. When we are told, "they came to the brook Eshcol," a place much nearer their encampment, it was on the return journey.

3. Their report of the land was enticing, their report of the inhabitants was terrifying. Giants dwelt in walled cities. "We are not able," said the spies, "to go up against the people, for they are stronger than we." This caused great excitement in the camp, and Caleb, one of the two spies, who did not agree with the latter part of the report, had to "still" the people before he could cry, "Let us go up at once and possess the land, for we are well able to overcome the inhabitants." The sins that we have to fight against are as formidable as these giants. The statement of the ten spies was imperfect rather than inaccurate: their report was true as far as it went, but their advice was bad. It seemed to them impossible to acquire the rich country, because of the mighty defenders; but Joshua and Caleb, while duly estimating the strength of the inhabitants, remembered the power of God, and all the wonders wrought by Him in the wilderness. In the spiritual combat we have to acknowledge that though without God we can do nothing good, yet with His assistance everything is possible.

The ten spies confessed the first, but forgot the second. Herein they are better than a good many men of the modern world, who, in their self-sufficiency, reject the proffered help of God, because they vainly suppose that they can lead a good life, and cultivate all the virtues, without His assistance. Men nowadays ignore the truth formulated in the tenth Article at the end of the Prayer Book, because it wounds their vanity. Nevertheless "we have no power to do good works pleasant and acceptable to God without the grace of God by Christ" first making us wish well, and secondly co-operating with us to work well. This is the truth which inspires the beautiful Collect for the Nineteenth Sunday after Trinity, " O God, forasmuch as without Thee we are not able to please Thee ; mercifully grant, that Thy Holy Spirit may in all things direct and rule our hearts ; through Jesus Christ our Lord." Amen.

This truth is enforced by the sequel of the story, which tells how the people rejected both counsels. They would neither confess their inability, nor trust in God, but invaded the land relying on their own strength, and were defeated.

4. The punishment for this rebellion is recorded very exactly in verse 34 of the next chapter, where we notice two points. First, the punishment was in no way arbitrary : it grew out of their course of action. The people said they would not, God said they should not, and the event proved they could not, which no doubt confirmed them in their opinion, and so they died under punishment, not because

The Investigation of the Spies. 73

God was harsh, but because they had to take the consequences of their own deeds.

Secondly, the punishment was accurately proportioned to their sin. Forty days of search, forty years of punishment. What this proportion is, in any case, none but God can fix, for none but He knows the full circumstances of the case, or can accurately estimate future results. But such a verse is meant to teach us that punishment is in no sense arbitrary, but most exactly fitted to the offence. Therefore we may leave it in the hands of so just a Judge, without grumbling, without expressing an opinion, feeling confident that He will do what is right.

CHAPTER IV., Sec. 2.

Monday.

THE INVESTIGATION OF GOD.

Ezek. xxxiv. 11 to 18 and John x. 1 to 19.

Notes :—

1. The idea of the Shepherd is a very old one, probably as old as the human race, for when we come to think of the food supply, we see at once that it is derived from two sources, from bread and from flesh; farms are of two kinds, tillage and pasture : there are two familiar figures on the face of the earth, the husbandman and the shepherd. It was so from the beginning, Cain and Abel followed these two employments, and both are used as figures to help us in knowing the divine character : God is our Shepherd and God is our Husbandman (John xv. 1).

2. There is something wonderfully attractive in the thought that God is seeking us. God said, through the prophet Ezekiel, "I will seek out My sheep," and Christ said, "The Son of Man is come to seek and to save that which was lost" (Luke xix. 10).

The Investigation of God. 75

Our salvation will be to the glory of God. If we may so put it, everything the Almighty does is for His own glory. If this was said of a man it would show most presumptuous conceit and utter selfishness. But it may be said of God, because whatever is done to His glory is done for the highest good; it is according to His own merits, and involves the greatest benefits to all creatures; whereas honour amongst us may be neither good for self nor for others. This may be seen in the case of King Saul, who asked Samuel to honour him before the people (1 Sam. xv. 25). It was not good for himself to receive what he had not deserved, and it was not good for the people to honour an undeserving sham.

3. The method is as exquisitely beautiful as the design. (*a*) The Good Shepherd "goeth before"; leads, not drives; He persuades, not compels. The picture is drawn in the East, where the shepherd walks first; not in the West, where he walks last, with a dog and a stick. (*b*) The Good Shepherd "calleth His own sheep by name," showing His individual knowledge and His study of character. We are not dealt with in the aggregate, but one by one. We can easily understand that discipline, which would brace a strong character, might crush a weak one. (*c*) The Good Shepherd gives freedom, for we "shall go in and out." The so-called Free Churches have parted with real liberty; trying to enter the Fold according to the rules of Booth,

Wesley and Co., they are the slaves of their founders. Christ has already laid down the plan embodied in the Catholic Church, and those who try to climb up some other way are sneaking thieves, or violent robbers. (*d*) The Good Shepherd does the best for His sheep. Everything that happens is best. "What is is best" *(Pope)*; not, of course, the best possible, but the best under the circumstances. The sheep "shall find pasture" now, and "shall be saved" hereafter. (*e*) The Good Shepherd "giveth His life for the sheep." It is the last thing He can do. It vindicates His absolute goodness. It makes His strong appeal. It will justify the reward of those who follow, and the punishment of those who turn a deaf ear to His voice.

4. This last remark brings us to a point explicitly stated by Ezekiel, but only implied by S. John—the Judgment. "I will judge between cattle and cattle"; rewards and punishments will be allotted even in this world. "I will feed them with judgment."

5. This allegory of the Good Shepherd, though so ancient, still colours our words and thoughts. Hymns are still addressed to our Lord in this character, and pictures are still painted of Him leading the flock, often with a lamb in His arms; and in the daily confession of sin we still say, "We have erred and strayed from Thy ways like lost sheep." In using any popular figure of speech it is perhaps necessary to be on our guard against unreality.

6. In John x. 16 it should be, "There shall be one *flock*," not one *fold*. We should pray and strive for the re-union of Christendom. It would be a great thing for the world if the three Churches of Greece, Rome, and England would mutually recognize each other, and agree not to invade one another's sphere of action: it would save a deal of discord, and a deal of labour, for they would then not interfere with each other, but would devote their efforts to converting the heathen. We don't want the Roman Mission in England. The Armenians don't want the Roman Mission in their country. We have no right to send a Protestant Mission to Spain, or to appoint a bishop of Jerusalem. But, on the other hand, it has been found impossible to work the Church from a single centre; nor is the national theory quite feasible. The best plan seems to be by that of Empire. The Eastern Empire under the Patriarchate of Constantinople; the Holy Roman Empire under the Pope. What, then, is to become of the two modern Empires of England and Russia? England has already solved the question, for all parts of her world-wide Empire are under the Patriarchate of Canterbury. In the East the problem is not yet worked out, for it remains to be seen whether Russia will form a new Patriarchate at Moscow, or whether the dream of Peter the Great will be realized, in the acquisition of Constantinople, and the revival of the ancient See in its full power.

CHAPTER IV., SEC. 3.

Tuesday.

THE INVESTIGATION OF MAN.
JER. XXIX. 13 and MATT. XIII. 44 to 47.

NOTES :—

1. Man's search after the Almighty is inspired by God Himself, for according to Article 10, to which we have already referred, "the condition of man after the Fall of Adam is such, that he cannot turn . . . himself . . . to calling upon God." God calls first and, as He always does call, the responsibility is thrown upon us. God calls, and if His voice finds any response in our breast, we answer. A welcome awaits us. When God called Adam he hid himself in the boscage of the garden ; but when God called Samuel, he answered readily and eagerly, "Speak! for Thy servant heareth." When two persons are seeking for each other, the probability is they will meet : so it is promised that if we seek "with all our heart" (Jer. xxix. 13), we shall find (See Deut. iv. 29).

2. This seeking should also be betimes. "Those

that seek Me early shall find Me." The morning of life should be consecrated to God's service. When life begins to dawn the infant is baptized; when the sun of intelligence has risen we are confirmed. The search after God goes on uninterruptedly; the knowledge of God, which *is* eternal life, accumulates steadily. It is very dangerous to postpone this search. The later it is begun, the less chance there is of success. It is very foolish to talk of young men sowing wild oats, with a smiling face, as if it would be all right by-and-bye, when, as a matter of course, they have turned over a new leaf. That is all nonsense, if a man sows the wind he will reap the whirlwind. If a man needs conversion, and puts it off, it becomes more difficult as time goes on. We do not say that death-bed repentance is impossible, but it is very rare. In the whole Bible there is only one instance, the dying thief; and the circumstances in which he found himself were peculiar and startling (see chap. ii., sec. 6).

3. This early seeking may also be understood of the morning. Moses, Joshua, Job, etc., rose early in the morning to worship God, so should we. The Church has encouraged the practice when she commands "fasting," and therefore early Communions. Many folks plead, "Sunday is the only morning in the week when we can lie in bed"; they should rather say, "Sunday is the only morning when we have the opportunity of getting up to worship God."

They should remember that it is impossible to sleep more than a certain number of hours, and the reason that they are so drowsy on a Sunday morning, is, probably, that they went gadding about on Saturday night to places of amusement, or to market, keeping tradesmen up late, and inflicting on them a day's work gigantic in its length. Let the Sacrificial Feast, which cost the Son of Man so much, cost us a little self-sacrifice in early rising when we attend it. We hear a lot of rubbish talked about the early Christians, let us look rather to the early performance of Christian duties.

4. This seeking must be done promptly. Sharpness is as valuable in religion as in business. Psalm xxvii. 9 teaches most beautifully that the heart should be sensitive in its quickness. The summons comes winsome in its affectionate invitation to the closest intimacy, " Seek ye My face." The answer springs instantaneously to the lips, " Thy face, Lord, will I seek." It is the voice and the echo.

5. This seeking brings prosperity, " Seek ye first the Kingdom of God and His righteousness, and all these things shall be added unto you " (Matt. vi. 33). A writer in the " Eastern Argus " once asked the pertinent question, Whether a good Christian was ever seen in rags and tatters? He suggested that Christianity properly applied would solve all the social problems of the day, and that it is better than all the nostrums of the faddists. It is an old-fashioned

but infallible remedy. I once heard a worthy East London vicar shouted down at a meeting of the clergy of his rural deanery, for saying that he did not believe in the existence of starving Christians! Yet I venture to think he was mainly right, for he had David on his side, who said, " I have been young, and now am old; and yet saw I never the righteous forsaken, nor his seed begging their bread" (Psalm xxxvii. 25).

6. Personal religion is the hid treasure, and the pearl of great price.

CHAPTER IV., Sec. 4.

Wednesday.

THE INVESTIGATION OF NATURE.
Rom. i. 18 to 23.

Notes :—

1. Natural religion consists in the spiritual and moral truths that may be gathered from a close study of the universe, which the Almighty, in making, left as a witness of His power, and organized as a proof of His wisdom. It first leads man to revealed religion, and afterwards corroborates that religion. The world has been called by Plato "God's Epistle," and the heathen are rebuked by S. Paul for not having read it rightly, as they might have done. This truth has been enshrined in one of those jewels of thought for which the Psalter is so famous—"The heavens are telling the glory of God, and the firmament showeth His handiwork" (xix. 1).

2. Many find the pursuit of natural science entrancing. It is indeed the handmaid of religion. Every secret that rewards the patient investigator is the gift of God. And every message received

The Investigation of Nature. 83

by the simple student from the songsters of the air, the flowers of the field, etc., is a message from God.

> "There is a book, who runs may read,
> Which heavenly truth imparts,
> And all the lore its scholars need,
> Pure eyes and Christian hearts."
> —*Keble.*

3. In our studies of nature, we must remember that "natural" when applied to the universe is good, but that "natural" when applied to man is bad. The reason of this is to be found in the Fall. Man so far fell from his natural state that sin became his second nature, whereas the universe was only slightly affected by that catastrophe, and though it became subject to vanity to some extent, it was not willingly. Grace, then, as things stand now, is supernatural.

4. In the passage we read to-day we are told that we may find hints of the eternity, the power, and the divinity of God. (*a*) Science has pushed her investigations back into the past and forward into the future without being able to discover the beginning or the end, which are to be found in God alone. (*b*) The vast extent of Nature, her infinite variety, her wonderful contrivances, and her marvellous adaptation of means to ends, demand that they should have been conceived and carried into effect by a God. (*c*) After viewing the world we may well cry, "I believe in God the Father Almighty."

5. Those who have seen the Alps cannot help but be impressed by their grandeur. Though the thoughts suggested by the hills be trite enough, they must occur to every thinking mind, when wandering and climbing amongst those natural sanctuaries, and they do us good. We protest against the flippant, not to say irreverent, observation of Mark Twain, that the Almighty having more land than He knew what to do with, stacked it! The idea is neither scientifically true, nor morally elevating. It is the degenerate offspring of a low wit.

6. This brings us to another point—grumbling at the weather, for which Englishmen are so famous. Our Continental neighbours laugh at us for our folly; it is more—it is a sin. I have listened to constant complaints from the same person that have been positively blasphemous. No sort of weather seems to suit. Then the expression "clerk of the weather" is a horrible profanity. Even when we put up the prayers of the Church for shine or rain, we should not indulge in bitter complaints at the evil we are suffering from, but endure it patiently as a visitation from Almighty God.

7. There are some obvious principles taught by nature that may be called elementary, and that we should not refer to here were they not so disregarded.

(a) Early hours. Early to bed, and early to rise. "An honest man goes to bed early like the west wind." The night is meant for sleep, and the day for work. Late hours are prejudicial to health; they are one of the great drawbacks of the invention of artificial light.

(b) Slowness in eating. Rapidity in gobbling up meals is almost a national failing in dyspeptic America. We call a lion ravenous, but see him fed at the Zoo, and we shall be astonished how slowly he eats.

(c) Moderation in eating and drinking. Sheridan once said to his friends after dinner, "Shall we drink like men or beasts?" "Like men," they cried with one voice, in horror. "Then we shall get jolly drunk," he replied, "for the beasts never take too much."

8. These teachings may be multiplied easily for ourselves. There remains only to record a warning, which is not unneeded nowadays. Nature seems to permit cruelty on a gigantic scale, Christianity teaches that it is a sin, and that the spirit of the sixth commandment must be extended to dumb animals. Further, Nature indulges in bitter enmity and furious fight, Christianity rather teaches love and peace.

CHAPTER IV., Sec. 5.

Thursday.

THE INVESTIGATION OF SCRIPTURE.
John v. 39 and Acts xvii. 11.

Notes :—

1. Once when on my parish rounds, an old man, who never thought of going to Church, boasted of having read the Bible through three times! It is not the quantity of Scripture read that benefits us, so much as the thoroughness and the prayerfulness with which we read. A single verse may suffice for meditation for a week.

2. It is said that every gentleman should know his Bible; we would rather say every Christian. The two verses suggested for to-day show us with what diligence the Jews searched their sacred writings.

(*a*) Whether we read "Search the Scriptures" with the A.V., or "Ye search the Scriptures" with the R.V., the general sense is much the same, *i.e.*, the well-known custom of studying the Bible is commended ; but if the verb is in the imperative,

The Investigation of Scripture. 87

as in the first case, we are told to do it more thoroughly than the Jews did.

(*b*) In the Acts it is recorded of the Bereans, to their praise, not only that they searched the Scriptures daily, but that they confirmed the preaching of the Apostles by the older revelation.

3. Protestant worship of the Bible has led more than anything else to its disuse. The Bible must be set in its proper place, and not made to usurp a position it was never meant to occupy. God has not left us with a dead book, like Mohamet left his followers with the Koran, but He has also given us a living Church, of which we are members. The Church is "the pillar of the truth" (1 Tim. iii. 15), not the Bible. The Church wrote the Bible, the Church has kept the Bible, and the Church alone has the right of interpretation. The Church, in matters of faith, is infallible and cannot err. That most people are totally unfitted to interpret the Bible for themselves, must be clear to every thoughtful mind, that recollects the absurd mistakes commonly made, *e.g.* (Psalm lxxxiv. 10), "A day in thy courts is better than a thousand" days there, which would be rather dull! Or again, because there is a mistranslation in the Baptismal Commission, as given in the A.V. of Matt. xxviii. 19, ignorant Dissenters, who do not know Greek, say that infants must not be baptized, because all candidates for Baptism have to be instructed first! They do not even take the

trouble to read the margin, where the correct translation is given.

4. A curious point in Bible reading is presented by the practice of the Board Schools. These Schools are distinguished for showing no favour to the Church, if not for direct opposition to her. We should therefore have thought that a translation of the Bible made by individuals would have been more acceptable than a translation made by the Church, but, as we shall see, it is not so. The irony of fate has decreed that they shall fall into the very trap they wished to avoid, as a punishment for their bigotry. The A.V. was made by a committee of Churchmen; the Great Bible, published in 1539, was merely a revision of the translation of Tyndal and Coverdale, two dissenting heretics. Now the Church, with a truly Catholic taste, perceiving that the Psalter and the Decalogue of the Great Bible were far the best, has retained that version in her Prayer Book, notwithstanding the tainted source from whence it came; while the School Board, on the other hand, to whom the Prayer Book is a sort of red rag before a bull, rejects the work of Dissenters contained therein in favour of the A.V. made by Churchmen, though these portions in it are not so good. From a literary point of view they are clearly wrong. "Thou shalt not kill" is not so good as "Thou shalt do no murder," neither so true nor so accurate, for killing

is not always murder. Then the English of the A.V. of the Psalter is neither so beautiful nor so musical as that of the Prayer Book. When we find boys and girls acquainted with the A.V. of these parts, and not the Prayer Book Version, we set them down as badly taught, not because we are Churchmen, but because we are critics.

5. The study of the Bible should proceed upon some system. The good old custom of encouraging boys and girls to read a few verses every day, which has fallen into disuse, might be revived. The Church provides several courses—the Sunday and week-day lessons, the daily recitation of the Psalter, and the series of Gospels and Epistles in the Missal. These latter are, of course, sung at High Mass, with the utmost care and elaboration, to glorify the Word of God. But there are many parts never read in public that may with advantage be studied in private, for even the stiffest books sparkle with gems of thought, graceful suggestions, and delicate hints, that have to be carefully sought.

CHAPTER IV., Sec. 6.

𝔉𝔯𝔦𝔡𝔞𝔶.

THE INVESTIGATION OF HISTORY.

EZRA IV. 11 to end.

NOTES :—

1. The Jews, under the decree of Cyrus, were rebuilding Jerusalem. The neighbouring people, not being allowed to assist at the work, because their heart was not right, wrote a malicious letter to Artaxerxes (Smerdis), representing that, if the city were rebuilt, it would be a danger to the empire. The malice of this letter may be estimated by their previous offer of assistance in rebuilding the very city whose new foundation they now objected to; and the wisdom of the rejection of their offer by Zerubbabel is brought out clearly by the falseness of their charge. The King had the *records* searched, and because he found that Jerusalem had been a mighty city in the days of old, he ordered the works to be stopped. In the reign of the next King, however, the contention of the Jews, that they worked under a decree of Cyrus, came once more into

prominence. The hostility of their enemies seems to have abated, for though they disliked the work, they are only anxious to be assured of the truth of the contention. Fresh search is made; the decree of Cyrus is found; and the Jews are allowed to continue the work. The point to be noticed is the search made into history by the Babylonian monarchs, which, in both cases, was made on the lines laid down in the letters addressed to them, and in both cases was successful, as far as it went, though in the first case it did not go far enough.

2. It is very instructive to search into the history of the Jews, because it is inspired, because it is history from God's point of view. The general tendency of the ages through which it runs is sketched, until we arrive at the Advent of Christ. Beside that, the incidents selected have been chosen each with a special moral purpose of its own, which the skilful teacher can draw out and apply for himself; therefore it is so necessary that the public shall be acquainted with these events, that they may recognize his allusions or his story; especially does a quotation lose point, and fall flat, if its exact place is not instantly known to the hearer.

3. The search for types also is exceedingly instructive, and is encouraged by our Lord and His Apostles, who often adduce them to illustrate events and teachings. The life of Joshua, *e.g.*, is a wonderful type of our Lord's life and work, and those scholars,

who learn the one, without being taught to recognize the other, have learnt to very little purpose, and will soon begin to ask, "*Cui bono?*"

4. This process is no less valuable in secular history, especially in these days of misrepresentation, when enemies of the press and Roman Catholicism have conspired to delude the public. A few examples may be taken.

(*a*) The Anglican Church is often called Protestant, both by her friends and foes. Even in the Coronation Oath, a State but not a Church document, it is so. No wonder that ignorant people accept this as true. But if a search be made into history it will be found utterly false, for never does the Church of England describe herself as Protestant.

(*b*) The Church of England separated from the Church of Rome! What a monstrous lie! We are not a sect; we never committed schism. It would be nearer the truth to say that the Church of Rome left us, when Pius V. published his famous bull, "*Regnans in excelsis,*" 1570.

(*c*) Henry VIII. was the first Protestant, who founded this Protestant Church of ours! Thus is history perverted by authors and newspaper writers. If this was true, the Church of England would have no right to pre-Reformation property; like the Presbyterians in Scotland have no right to the property on which they have laid their sacrilegious hands.

(*d*) The Reformation is generally represented as

The Investigation of History. 93

an unmixed blessing, while the real truth is that it was a great calamity.

Let an appeal be made to history. Let the truth be discovered by competent scholars. We stand at the judgment bar of God, Who directs the affairs of the world.

CHAPTER IV., Sec. 7.

Saturday.

THE INVESTIGATION OF THE HEART.

Ps. LXXVII. 5, 6 *(P.B.V.)*; Lam. III. 40, 41 ; 1 Cor. XI. 28.

Notes :—

1. There is one petition in the Litany which comes very acceptably to most people, viz., "That it may please Thee to give us true repentance; to forgive us all our sins, negligences, and ignorances," etc. They put a delightfully broad and easy construction upon the word "ignorances," that it will not bear. Instead of pleading for their sins of ignorance, they plead for ignorance of their sins; in a word, they ask forgiveness for all their sins, but what those sins are they have not the least idea! A woman once announced candidly in my presence that she was as good as she could be! When I exclaimed, "I'm sorry to hear it!" she was vastly surprised. But, of course, on her own showing, she was one of those self-deceivers of whom S. John speaks, who have no need of the Saviour.

The Investigation of the Heart.

Once I interrogated a youth whom I knew very well upon the subject.

" Do you go to Confession ? "

" No ! " said he, " I should not know what to confess ! "

" Have you done no sins ? " I asked.

" Oh, yes ! " said he ; " but I'm sure I don't know what they are." Yet, when I put him a few test questions, it soon became apparent that he had broken the whole Decalogue.

2. In chap. ii., sec. 7, we considered the power of Absolution as it was committed to the Church, we will consider to-day one of the benefits of auricular Confession. It is self-knowledge. "Know thyself" was the famous advice of the oracle at Delphi. How far self-knowledge extends we may judge from our own experience and that of others. The two cases just given are but examples from the general state of affairs. Most men do not know themselves. The neglect of Confession is answerable for much of this ignorance of self, which is so disastrous to our spiritual progress. We do not obtain forgiveness for those sins we never confess. It is of no use saying God reads the heart, as an excuse for not reading it ourselves. We must be able to say clearly and definitely what our sins are, else we can never be sorry for them, or turn over a new leaf; *i.e.*, Repentance is impossible. If, on the other hand, we are in the habit of going to Confession, the

priest, unlike the Almighty, does not know our sins till we tell him, and we cannot tell him until we know ourselves.

The other two chief benefits of Confession are the advice we get from a priest trained to give it, and sacramental absolution of which we are assured.

3. Asaph, in Psalm lxxvii., alludes to a retrospect covering a considerable period of time. Jeremiah, in Lamentations, reveals a state of things in Judæa very much the same as in the England of to-day, a general ignorance of self. S. Paul insists on a strict self-examination before making communions.

4. The first part of the Missal is preparatory; therefore the office begins with the Decalogue, on which we are supposed to have questioned ourselves previously. The Commandments are the lines on which it is suggested that we hold enquiry into our character. A few questions based on the Commandments may be found useful.

    (1) Does God hold the chief place in our regard? or do we think more of ourselves, our money, our pleasure?

    (2) Do we worship God in the right way? *i.e.*, at Church, or do we flirt with Dissent?

    (3) Are we strictly truthful? Do we set a guard on our lips?

    (4) Do we spend our time well?—in worship on Sunday? at work during the week?

The Investigation of the Heart.

(5) Do we obey God in all things? Do we obey His representatives in the home, in the school, in the State, in the Church?

(6) Do we hate anyone? Are we good tempered? Are we kind?

(7) Are we pure? Are we clean? Are we sober?

(8) Are we honest?

(9) Do we guard our neighbour's character as jealously as we guard our own? Do we like gossiping? If we have nothing good to say of our neighbour, do we keep the bad to ourselves?

(10) Are we greedy? covetous? and, if so, idolatrous?

The Holy Spirit will help us to use and multiply these tests.

CHAPTER V., Sec. 1.

𝔉ourth 𝔖unday.

THE REVELATION OF LAW.

Exod. xxiv. 12 to end.

NOTES :—

1. Imagine the scene: the mountain rearing its rocky sides into the heavens; the fence about the foot, beyond which the trembling people might not venture, on pain of death; the storm; the cloud-crowned summit; the darkness; the thunder and lightning; the fire; the piercing voice like the sound of a trumpet; and the Revelation.

2. Moses was absent forty days and forty nights; when he returned to the camp the people were worshipping the golden calf with divine rites; in his indignation and wrath he cast the tablets of the Law to the ground, so that they were broken to pieces, as a symbol of the national apostasy. After this he had to return to the mount for another copy, and was again absent forty days and forty nights. When he came once more amongst the people his face shone with the glow of a divine radiancy, as befitted

one privileged to hold such close intercourse with God, and commissioned to vindicate the majesty of the Law. "The people were afraid to come nigh him" (Exod. xxxiv. 30); but this was not the reason for veiling his face. The light was only transitory; therefore he veiled his face, that the people might not see it was a glory gradually passing away (consult 2 Cor. iii. 7, R.V.).

3. The tablets were probably of the hard red granite of the district. This may be taken as a type of the heart, which is stony (Ezek. xi. 19) and hard (Ezek. iii. 7). The new covenant is, however, to be engraved on the heart (2 Cor. iii. 3). These tablets were inscribed on both sides (Exod. xxxii. 15), which may teach us that our religion should be thorough, in public and in private, before God and man alike; we must be without dissimulation, honest, genuine, not double-faced.

4. As to the division, the two tables contained the two duties—to God and man. This is sanctioned by Christ. But there are two further questions.

(a) Where are the Commandments divided? The right answer is to be found in the Catechism. The Church of Rome joins the first and second, and then, to make up the number, divides the tenth. To join the first and second is to confuse atheism and polytheism—too much religion with none at all; while to divide the tenth is to make a distinction without a difference.

(*b*) A far more important question is, where are the tablets to be divided? Undoubtedly there were five commandments on each tablet. This is not the place to enter into the arguments; a text book had better be consulted for them; but see what a noble result! What a halo of divinity is cast over the persons we are bound to obey, if the fifth Commandment is part of the duty to God. The father rules in the family, the master rules in the school, the monarch rules in the State, the bishop rules in the Church, each by divine right, each is God's representative in his own sphere.

5. Notice the position of the Decalogue in the Catechism! As body without spirit is dead, so faith without works is dead, therefore the Decalogue follows the Creed, and is obligatory on us under our third baptismal vow of obedience.

6. From the last remark it follows that if there is no vow we are not bound to obey! However much this may startle some it is strictly true, and is a reason of the very greatest weight in favour of infant Baptism. If the child has been baptized, there is at once a ground of appeal; it has received the privileges, it is bound to perform the duties; but if the child has not been baptized, what becomes of the obligation? There is none. The parent may say, "Do this to please me," but if the child hates its parents, as is often the case, it laughs at the command.

7. God is the Source of all authority; therefore

every good citizen is under a moral obligation to obey the laws of the community in which he lives, unless they clash with a higher law, in which case he should suffer death rather than obey. If the quality of a law is a matter of opinion, he is at liberty to get it amended or repealed by legitimate means. In like manner we are bound to obey the Church.

8. The Law is summed up in the all-powerful virtue of Love (see Rom. xiii. 10). If we love God we shall do the first duty, and if we love our neighbour we shall perform the second. Iron becomes soft when melted by fire; hearts become obedient when fired by Love.

CHAPTER V., Sec. 2.

Monday.

THE REVELATION OF GOD.

Exod. iii. 1 to 16.

Notes :—

1. A fire in a bush is a much more startling contrast in a dry desert than in a fertile country like our own. The wonder was that it was not consumed in a moment. This miracle has been taken as a type of the Incarnation. Certainly the circumstances are strikingly parallel. The presence of God was localized; He came down as fire upon that fragile bush without doing it an injury: in like manner God, "Who is a consuming fire," became Incarnate when the Holy Ghost came upon S. Mary, and the power of the Highest overshadowed her, without ruining her frail body, or spoiling the delicate bloom of her maidenhood. Both miracles took place secretly, without observation from the world, and both brought salvation to the Church.

2. The revelation of God seems to have been gradual. In the English Bible there is a distinct

system of printing observed in rendering the Divine Name.

(*a*) God (Elohim). The strong One, distinguished for his power, the Almighty Creator, Whom we fear and worship, because of his omnipotence. The original word is in the plural number, which we may perhaps accept, on the authority of some commentators, as a faint indication of plurality in the Godhead,—an adumbration of the existence of the Trinity, Who was afterwards to be more fully revealed.

(*b*) LORD (Jehovah). The Eternal Being, the Self-existent, "the God of development" or "evolution" (*Kurtz*). This Name is supposed to contain a more advanced revelation. It was the Name of the Burning Bush. It was the most sacred Name among the Jews, which, as we have seen (chap. iii., sec. 3), they would not employ on ordinary occasions, preferring to substitute some other title, which will account for them taking up stones when our Lord said, "Before Moses was I am."

(*c*) GOD (Jehovah). This great Name is rendered both by LORD and GOD, according to the set of vowels employed in the Hebrew.

(*d*) Lord. The Ruler, the Sovereign, the Monarch. In English the word means loaf-giver. So we may say it is the King who rules for the benefit of his subjects, that they may have life, and having life may have it abundantly.

3. In the first of the thirty-nine Articles, God is described as a Being "without body, parts, or passions," in other words, a Spirit. But such is the infirmity of language, owing to the limitation of conception, that we are wont to speak of the Almighty in terms which would imply that He was a man, did we not start by stating that He is a Spirit. Such language is abundant in the Bible; we speak of the "eye of God" because we cannot express seeing without the organ of sight. In fact, an eye by itself has become a symbol of Godhead, and is often so used in pictures, etc. The "stretched out arm," by which the Almighty is said to save his people, is merely a figure of speech signifying strength. In the same way the "hand of the Lord" implies his justice in rewarding and punishing, sometimes his power in protecting, *e.g.*, "No man is able to pluck them out of my Father's hand" (John x. 29), etc. In paintings the Almighty is often represented as an old man. This expresses his hoary antiquity, He is "from everlasting," but it conveys no idea of his eternal youth, for He is "to everlasting"; if without beginning also without end. In several places of the Old Testament, *e.g.*, when He appeared to Joshua, He assumed the very appearance of a man, which we may regard, in the light of the future, as previous hints of the Incarnation.

4. The final revelation of God is the revelation of the Blessed Trinity, which is fixed in

the threefold division of the Creed. I believe—
- (*a*) In God the Father, Who hath made me and all the world.
- (*b*) In God the Son, Who hath redeemed me and all mankind.
- (*c*) In God the Holy Ghost, Who sanctifieth me and all the elect.

CHAPTER V., SEC. 3.

Tuesday.

THE REVELATION OF SIN.

Rom. v. 12 to end, and vii. 7 to 14.

NOTES:—

1. As ignorance is not innocence, so it is necessary to study sin if we would aim at holiness. It is necessary to study the nature of sin before conscience, working under the influence of the Holy Spirit, will convict us of it. It is not enough to avoid sin; we must hate it with a perfect hatred—it must be repulsive to us, until we reach that infinitely exalted attitude of the Almighty Himself, Who is "of purer eyes than to behold iniquity."

2. Sin is original and actual, *i.e.*, personal. By original sin we mean that tendency to evil with which we were born, and which causes even the smallest child to make unpleasant exhibitions of its ugly nature before its will is sufficiently developed to act consciously. It does not matter just here how we acquired original sin, experience tells us that

we've got it. The Sacrament of Baptism takes away its guilt, though not its consequences; therefore we say, "I believe in one Baptism for the remission of sins." ACTUAL sin is what we do wrong when we distinctly wish. In Baptism adults may obtain remission of actual sins up to that moment. But after Baptism we must seek forgiveness of sin in penance, whether sacramental or not, according to what was set forth in chap. iv., sec. 7.

3. Actual sin is mortal, *i.e.*, deadly, or venial. All sins are not equal, some are worse than others. This difference is pointed out by S. John in 1 John v. 16—"A sin which is not unto death," and "a sin unto death," and by our Lord when He compared some sins to a mote, others to a beam. The following are the seven deadly sins, with the opposite virtues:—

Pride.	Humility.
Covetousness.	Liberality.
Lust.	Charity.
Anger.	Meekness.
Gluttony.	Temperance.
Envy.	Brotherly love.
Sloth.	Diligence.

4. Punishment is fixed by God in proportion to the sin. Even under human governments the same penalty is not awarded to every offence. In their dealings with sin there are two most important points of difference between the human and the

Divine governments: under the Divine system, as administered by God, the punishment is exactly proportioned to the offence, and every sin is punished. Even if we obtain forgiveness the punishment must follow to purge us from its stain. What a man soweth that *shall* he also reap. Hence it follows that penitents will go to Purgatory when they die, to be thoroughly purged, by undergoing the necessary corrective punishment.

5. Many instructive names are used to describe sins.

(*a*) *Sin.* This is the native Anglo-Saxon word that comes naturally to us, and needs no explanation. It is the general word.

(*b*) *Transgression.* A crossing the boundary-line between right and wrong.

(*c*) *Trespass.* Also a going over.

(*d*) *Unrighteousness.* A negative term, to be without righteousness.

(*e*) *Iniquity.* That which is not equal; that which has not come up to the required standard. Both sins and virtues are described under this figure. That which is virtuous is equal—" Let thine eyes look upon the thing that is equal " (Psalm xvii. 2), and that which is sinful is unequal—" Their way is not equal " (Ezek. xxxiii. 17).

(*f*) *Offence.* That which strikes or grates against God, that which displeases Him, shocks Him, grieves Him, makes Him angry.

(g) *Fault.* A flaw, a blemish, a defect. The real meaning of the word comes out in the expression, "at fault," *i.e.*, puzzled, deceived. We should acknowledge our sins, "not dissemble, nor cloke them, before the face of Almighty God our Heavenly Father."

(h) *Wrong.* The opposite to right. That which has been wrested.

(i) *Debt.* Something unpaid that we owe to God: duty undone.

(j) *Vice.* A fault, an imperfection. The opposite of virtue, which primarily means strength, showing that sin is a weakness, which can only be overcome by Divine assistance, called grace—that is never refused when asked for, and is even anticipated by the goodness of God, Who prompts the asking.

6. There are many classifications of sin, which are helpful.

   (a) *Sins of commission*—breach of negative precepts—a going beyond—transgression.
      Sins of omission—breach of positive precepts—a coming short of—iniquity.

   (b) *Sins of the world*—slander, show, greed.
       ,,   ,, *flesh*—lust, sloth, drunkenness.
       ,,   ,, *devil*—pride, lying, murder.

   (c) *Sins against God*
       ,,   ,, *neighbour* } may we live { a godly, righteous and sober } life.
       ,,   ,, *self*

(d) *Sins of thought*—malice, hatred.
　　　„　*word*—swearing.
　　　„　*deed*—murder.

7. S. Paul says, "I had not known sin but by the law." God's laws are not arbitrary; they are founded upon eternal principles. We can always distinguish a sin from a virtue by its effects, whether they are good or bad.

CHAPTER V., Sec. 4.

Wednesday.

THE REVELATION OF LOVE.

1 Cor. XIII.

Notes :—

1. God is a Spirit, in Himself Love, in His manifestation Light. His thoughts, words, and deeds all spring from this mighty source, which orders the universe, and regulates the world. Therefore the revelation of God is the revelation of Love.

2. "So God loved the world, that He gave His only-begotten Son, to the end that all who believe in Him should not perish, but have everlasting life." This is the second of the "comfortable words" in the Missal. So great was the love of God that He gave, if we may say so, not Himself, but His only Son. His full wish for mankind, which may be accomplished, we doubt not, in some far distant age, is, that they may all share everlasting life. It is not God that condemns sinners; they condemn themselves by their own sins.

3. Our Saviour carried this Love one stage further

when He declared, "Greater love hath no man than this, that a man lay down his life for his friends" (John xv. 13), and when He afterwards illustrated His own saying by His own death—a death of intense suffering.

4. The Holy Spirit of God loves us no less than the Father and the Son. So great is His regard for our true interest that He convicts us of sin; so intimate is His relation to us that He comforts us, both in the sense of consoling us in sorrow, and strengthening us in weakness; and so susceptible is His tenderness that He is said to grieve at our waywardness.

5. Love is revealed in Marriage. In the earlier ages of the world any motive rather than Love influenced these contracts, and it is recorded, as we have seen, as an astonishing exception that Isaac "loved" Rebekah. When marriage was raised to be a Sacrament, the outward and visible sign conveyed the inward and spiritual grace of graces—Love. When Christ pronounced the absolute indissolubility of marriage, He enforced Love as the all-embracing motive. If men married for expediency, say, their motive might disappear under changed circumstances, and a divorce might become possible; but if men married from Love, the motive of Love being eternal, could never change, and, therefore, not only did marriage become indissoluble to them, but to others also, that Love might be protected, and

that men who had not submitted to her holy influence might be punished.

6. Love is revealed in Friendship. This is the greatest revelation of Love outside the Being of God Himself. The love of Jonathan for David, which is a typical instance of its kind, "passed the love of women." On behalf of his friend, with whom he was on the most affectionate terms, he was ready to waive his right to the crown, and though he was removed by death his willingness was no less real. The very name, David, is perhaps not a name at all, but a term of endearment, meaning "darling," in which the name of Israel's greatest king has been swallowed up. Solomon witnessed to the existence of the same transcendent affection when he wrote, "There is a friend (*i.e.*, a lover) that sticketh closer than a brother" (Prov. xviii. 24). And Solomon, with all his opportunities of choice, failed to find a woman he could love, but succeeded in finding a man to fill the vacant throne of his heart, though, unfortunately, his name has not been preserved—"One man among a thousand have I found, but a woman among all those have I not found" (Eccles. vii. 28). In the New Testament we find S. John standing in the closest and tenderest relationship to our Lord, and called the Beloved Disciple.

7. Amongst the Jews marriage was the highest ideal state, because in some family the Messiah was to be born, and happy that family, and blessed

amongst women, that Mother, who should be found worthy of such an honour. But amongst Christians celibacy has ever been held the highest ideal state; so we read that when S. John had his vision of Heaven, and saw the Lamb standing on Mount Zion, in His presence was a select company of 144,000, as well as a general multitude, which no man could number. The select company are the celibates, the first-fruits, who follow the Lamb "whithersoever He goeth," while the numberless multitude are those Christians who have adopted the lower standard of marriage, "which Christ adorned and beautified with His presence and first miracle that He wrought in Cana of Galilee." (See Rev. xiv. 1-6.)

8. The great test of all genuine love is attending the Eucharist at least once on Sundays, and other days of obligation—attending the commemorative sacrifice of Love. We are told to "do this in remembrance of Me": if we do it not we have no Love; and without Love we shall go down into hell.

9. Works of charity are the outward expressions of the celestial grace. Hospitals are works of charity, and therein is their merit: if they were supported from the rates, and subject to public control, they would lose the value of this their special characteristic. Education used to be on this footing, but, alas, is so no longer in a great many cases. So great is men's lack of Love, nay, so great is their hatred of Love,

that to be a charity school child is looked down upon as a degradation!

10. 1 Cor. xiii., the noblest panegyric ever written on Love, opens with an astonishing statement of its surpassing worth. If I have, says S. Paul, the gift you think greatest—tongues; or if I have the gift I think greatest—interpretation; or if I have that gift on which Christ laid so much stress—Faith; or if I have the outward acts of Love without the principle, I am nothing. The all-permeating gift itself is the one thing without which everything else is worthless. The Apostle then descends, as it were, from these sublime assertions to describe the nature of this wonderful virtue. Can anything else be added, or must the conclusion be comparatively tame? Yes, he can soar again to the highest Heaven in the final declaration of the immortality of Love.

11. "O Lord, Who hast taught us that all our doings without charity are nothing worth; send Thy Holy Ghost, and pour into our hearts that most excellent gift of charity, the very bond of peace and of all virtues, without which whosoever liveth is counted dead before Thee. Grant this for Thine only Son Jesus Christ's sake." *Amen.*

CHAPTER V., Sec. 5.

Thursday.

THE REVELATION OF CHRIST IN THE CHURCH.

Eph. i. 15 to end.

Notes :—

1. Once when visiting in Northampton, a woman, who believed herself to be very religious, asked me to talk about the Lord Jesus. I instinctively felt what she wanted—all the pious commonplaces in which Dissenters delight, and I as instinctively rebelled against giving her stones for bread; so I talked of the manner in which Christ revealed Himself in the "Church, which is His Body." At last, interrupting me, she cried, "I asked you to tell me of Jesus, and you keep on talking of the Church." "Yes," I replied, "I thought I would tell you of that part of the Gospel which I knew you had forgotten." By this time she had quite lost her temper, so wishing her quietly good-day, I left her to think over what I had said.

2. Now S. Paul's prayer for the Saints at Ephesus

was, that God would give them "the spirit of wisdom ... in the knowledge of Him," and one of the points on which he wished them to be perfectly enlightened was, how Christ was Head of the Church, how the Church was the Body of Christ, and "the fulness of Him that filleth all in all."

3. The figures of speech employed to teach us the relationship of Christ and the Church are threefold, revealing a relationship close, closer, closest. (*a*) A binding contact, as in the figure of the temple, and the foundation or the corner-stone, supporting, finishing, ornamenting, attaching part to part in one homogeneous whole. (*b*) A personal contact, as in the very common figure of the king ruling his subjects and administering the law. (*c*) A life-giving contact, such as that of the vine and the branches living by the sap that glides up through the fibres, and yielding a most delicious fruit; or the still more appropriate figure of the body, which hints at the fact that the Church is the most masterly of the spiritual creations of God.

4. There is another most beautiful figure used in the fifth chapter of this very Epistle to describe the mysterious relationship—that of the Bride. It is very little understood; perhaps we could scarcely expect that men, who fail to grasp how husband and wife are one, should comprehend how Christ and the Church are one. Really, as the wife is the second half or complement of her husband, so the

Church is "the fulness of Him that filleth all in all."

5. The union of Christ and the Church is mysterious, the Church is "the mystical body." It is equally true to say that Christ dwells in us, and that we dwell in Him (John xv. 5). In some mysterious way He imparts to us the principle of life, so that our life becomes His life. Union with Him is life; separation from Him is death.

6. This union is, of course, begun in Baptism, strengthened at Confirmation, renewed by each Communion, broken by sin, and restored by penance. This is what is meant by the Communion, or common union, of Saints, by which they have fellowship with one another, and with each of the Persons of the Blessed Trinity, the union with our Lord being the closest, owing to the Incarnation. We are sons of the Father, but members of the Son.

7. Hence it happens that our lives in their different manifestations are mirrors of His Life. His transcendent attributes are, to a certain extent, reproduced by ourselves. The worth of any individual is estimated by God according to the amount of vitality which Christ is able to impart. By His power the intellect is quickened, the heart is warmed, the holiness is deepened, the sympathy is broadened, the energy is strengthened. Thus we trace Christ in His Saints, and He is "glorified in them" (John xvii. 10). If the promise, "Lo, I am with you always, even unto the end of the world," is true in a

particular sense of the Apostolical Succession, it is no less true, though in a different and general sense, for the whole assembly, who receive the Sacraments.

8. As we get to know our friends by their possessions, so we know Christ in the Church, which is His great possession in this world, bought with the price of His precious Blood. There are two words used as the name of Christ's great society. (*a*) Our word "Church," which means "of or belonging to the Lord," and lays stress on the nearness and dearness of the possession. (*b*) The Romance word of the French and Italian languages, etc., which means an assembly, and lays stress on the vastness and the grandeur of His possession.

CHAPTER V., Sec. 6.

Friday.

THE REVELATION OF THE REAL PRESENCE.

1 Cor xi. 23 to 33.

NOTES:—

1. The infinite importance of the Eucharist is most signally emphasized by this special revelation of its institution to S. Paul, as one of the leading Apostles. The Almighty, in His wisdom, considered that this, the only Christian Service commanded in the New Testament, should be communicated by a direct revelation to the great European missionary, rather than that he should receive an account of it second-hand, even from those who were present on the solemn occasion. The Lord Himself interposed in the conversion of this man of genius, and He again interposed to instruct him on the reality of the Presence, and in the essentials of saying the Office. We are told of the first interposition on the way to Damascus, about 36 A.D. Is there any further mention of the second except in this passage?

Revelation of the Real Presence. 121

Perhaps it was at the time of the "revelations of the Lord," in which he gloried, when he was caught up into Paradise, and "heard unspeakable words, which it is not lawful for a man to utter" (2 Cor. xii. 4). This took place in 43 A.D., before his ordination. The original word for "lawful" signifies authorization. No man is allowed to make use of these words but a priest only.

2. We judge so far of the importance of the service from this special revelation, and from the special command of our Lord to observe it, and to this we may add the recorded practice of Apostolic times; with this, before going further, we may contrast the practice of some amongst ourselves. In many churches the Eucharist is not even celebrated weekly, much less daily, as the Prayer Book provides. In many more churches it is not made the chief service of the day, by being fixed at the usual hour for church-going, and by being rendered with more dignity of ritual and music than the other services. We all know, to our shame and grief, how Matins and Evensong have usurped its place in the minds of the faithless clergy, and in the affections of the forgetful people.

3. The secret of the importance of this service lies in the Real Presence. When our Lord instituted the Eucharist He said, "THIS IS MY BODY, and this IS MY BLOOD," words which He repeated when He made the memorable communication to S. Paul.

Again, when our Lord preached His famous sermon on the Bread of Life, in the synagogue at Capernaum, He spoke of eating His flesh, and drinking His blood, saying, "The Bread which I *will* give is My flesh," etc. His meaning was unmistakable. The Jews "strove" with one another. He repeated His words; He did not explain them away. They were accounted "a hard saying," at which many "stumbled." From that time many of His disciples went back and walked no more with Him." He gave the chosen Twelve, who were definitely committed to Him, the opportunity of departing also. And He could no longer walk in Judæa, because the Jews sought to kill Him.

In our Prayer Book the same words are repeated by the priest, authorized to repeat them, at every Consecration. Bread and Wine are placed on the Altar, at the bidding of the priest they are changed, so that the Body and Blood are given to the Communicants. This same truth is taught in the Catechism. It is also expressed very clearly in Art. xxviii., which states that the Body of Christ is not only eaten in the Sacrament, but also "given" and "taken." In other words, the Presence is objective, local, Real, though spiritual. The Church of England does not attempt to explain this mystery, the Church of Rome does, and her theory is called "Transubstantiation," of which the doctrine of the Real Presence is quite independent.

The finest wheat bread, and the purest fermented wine must be provided for the purpose. Silver vessels bear it. Fine linen covers it. Every crumb and every drop of its outward form must be carefully consumed at once, except that which is to be Reserved in the Tabernacle for worship.

4. The Real Presence is the basis of all ritual, and the primary motive of church-going. The King sits upon His Altar Throne, and His people flock to His Courts to attend His reception, like they flock to the court of an earthly monarch. At the time of the first enunciation of the doctrine many found it too hard to believe; it is the same now. That it is not firmly believed and sufficiently taught accounts for irregularity of attendance at church on the one hand, and non-attendance on the other. We shall never witness a revival of religion to any extent until these five customs are universally adopted in every church:—

(a) A weekly, and, if possible, a daily Eucharist, to show its importance.

(b) An ornate service, to show its dignity.

(c) The reserved Sacrament,
(d) Open Churches, } to give a constant opportunity of worship.

(e) These practices enforced by constant teaching.

CHAPTER V., Sec. 7.

Saturday.

THE REVELATION OF HEAVEN.
Rev. xxi.

Notes :—

1. We begin our eternal life here. "He that heareth My Word, and believeth Him that sent Me, *hath* eternal life"—*hath*, not shall have, but hath it now (John v. 24). This needs the strongest affirmation, so we read again, "Verily, verily, I say unto you, he that believeth on Me *hath* eternal life" (John vi. 47). It is received, not inherited with the immortality of the soul, "the free gift of God is eternal life in Christ Jesus our Lord" (Rom. vi. 23). It consists, as we are told in the second Collect for the day, in knowledge of God, not in knowing about God, which is a very different thing, but in knowing God. "This is life eternal, that they should know Thee, the true God, and Jesus Christ Whom Thou hast sent" (John xvii. 3). Yet, though we have it now, we have still to look forward to it as future; like S. Paul, we live "in hope of eternal life" (Tit.

The Revelation of Heaven.

i. 2). It is progressive in its nature, and will not attain its final consummation until we get to Heaven, "in the world to come eternal life" (Mark x. 30). We qualify by making the great renunciation (Mark x. 29). The means by which we receive it is frequent Communion, " He that eateth My flesh, and drinketh My blood hath eternal life " (John vi. 54).

2. It need scarcely be said that the expressions, " Kingdom of God," and " Kingdom of Heaven," always refer to some aspect of religion in this world, whether personal or corporate—to some aspect of the Holy Catholic Church, membership of which carries with it the inheritance of eternal life, if not forfeited. Our salvation depends on our relation to the Church.

3. Our natural body is so different to what our spiritual body will be, that it makes it difficult for us to picture to ourselves Heaven. Our joy, however, will be rapturous, our satisfaction complete, our wildest expectations surpassed, our rest unruffled, and all the possibilities of our being will blossom to their perfect development.

It may be described negatively. There will be no sin. Therefore all the sad and bitter consequences of sin will be absent. Just think what that means! There will be no sorrow, no tears, no pain, no suffering, no death. We shall be no longer terrified by guilty fears, nor distracted by unbelief; we shall no longer be defiled by impurity, or outraged by murder and fornication; we shall no longer try to overreach our neighbours by cunning sorceries, nor shall we deceive ourselves in turn by crafty lies, nor shall we be deceived by some idol to which we have surrendered the liberty we did not appreciate.

It may be described positively. It is the vision of God, the reward of the sincere, the blessing of the pure-hearted (Matt. v. 8). Our "eyes shall see the King is His beauty" (Isa. xxxiii. 17). There will be perpetual light in the presence of God, and exhaustless pleasures for evermore in His company (Psalm xvi. 12). There will be complete knowledge, for we shall know even as we are known (1 Cor. xiii. 12), and a boundless love that is eternal, for God is Love, as He is Light.

4. We shall not be all equal in Heaven, any more than we are all equal here, for we shall differ in glory as star differs from star (1 Cor. xv. 41 and 42). Yet we shall be perfectly happy, for each one will be completely satisfied. The old illustration of the glasses is an admirable one: a number of tumblers of different sizes may be all full of water, yet the quantity is different in each case, and varies with the capacity. In Heaven each one will have as much happiness as he requires.

5. The statement that "we brought nothing into this world, neither may we carry anything out," refers entirely to material possessions, for S. John says, "The kings of the earth shall bring their glory

and honour into it" (Rev. xxi. 24); and national achievements shall be carried thither, for "they shall bring the glory and honour of the nations into it" (Rev. xxi. 26); and individual reputation will be there, for the blessing of those who die in the Lord is not only rest, but also fame (Rev. xiv. 13).

6. "There is no respect of persons with God" (Rom. ii. 11) does not mean that He will show no favouritism, for He will indeed grant the highest favours to the most deserving. The word refers to the masks which were worn by the actors in the Greek theatres, behind which they hid their faces. And God, Who is a righteous Judge, will strip off the mask of dissimulation, and make our real selves to appear before He passes sentence.

7. The revelation of hell is the antithesis of the revelation of Heaven. Darkness for light; weeping and wailing for rejoicing; and gnashing of teeth, impotent rage, for supreme contentment.

8. "O God, Who hast prepared for them that love Thee such good things as pass man's understanding; Pour into our hearts such love towards Thee, that we, loving Thee above all things, may obtain Thy promises, which exceed all that we can desire, through Jesus Christ our Lord." *Amen.*

CHAPTER VI., Sec. 1.

Fifth Sunday.

THE PUNISHMENT OF THE WORLD.

GEN. VI., VII. and VIII.

NOTES :—

1. The Flood was probably only a partial catastrophe, and did not extend over the whole surface of the earth. But since it destroyed all mankind, with the exception of the favoured few, it is not at all surprising that the impression made upon their minds was that it was universal, and that this impression was reproduced in their account of it, even in that account which we have in Scripture, for it was nothing to God's purpose to correct such an impression. He wished to emphasize the destruction of the human race, and so the extent of the Flood was immaterial. There are several impressions of this sort in the Bible, on subjects with which it is not concerned—*e.g.*, in Job xxvi. 11 the earth is represented as a flat plain supporting the hemisphere of the sky on pillars, as it appeared to the imperfect observations of primitive man. Though

utterly false in fact, it is a valuable witness to the imperfect state of science in those early days. The Bible does not aim at teaching astronomy, and therefore left the theory alone, which in no way vitiates what it does intend to teach, except in the opinion of ignorant man. A theologian may preach a sermon, and in preaching may take an illustration from, or allude to, some subject he does not understand. In doing this he may make a mistake; if an ignorant man happens to detect the mistake he will think nothing of the teaching of the sermon, which, in his case, will entirely miss the mark, while the student will be able to value the truth, though rejecting the inaccuracy.

2. The state of the world in the days of Noah was a terrible one. Every imagination of the thoughts of man's heart was only evil continually. Religion was entirely banished, for men, according to their own ideas, could live very agreeably without it. They had apostasized. Feasting and marrying occupied their time pleasantly enough. Everyone said to himself, like the rich fool in the parable, "Take thine ease, eat, drink, and be merry" (Luke xii. 19), until God said to each individual, with the special emphasis of sure and certain destruction, "Thou fool, this night thy soul shall be required of thee." Violence also filled the earth. It is a state of society which our Lord said would be found at the end of the world. Men would be living in fancied security,

enjoying the passing moment, saying that might is right, and feeling strong in the exercise of their power, when suddenly the Son of Man will appear bringing destruction. We seem to be verging towards such a state nowadays. As Tennyson says in "In Memoriam" "Women and cards and wine," *i.e.*, lust, eating and amusement, fill up the entire lives of thousands. The body is fed but not wisely, the mind is fed but not extensively, and the soul is starved.

3. In 2 Peter ii. 5 Noah is called "a preacher of righteousness." The Flood seems to have been announced one hundred and twenty years before it came, during which period Noah preached righteousness and threatened calamity; but his words fell unheeded on the ears of the men of his generation; they would not listen to his warning. Having thrown this chance away, God in His long-suffering gives them another seven days for repentance, after Noah had entered the ark, and before the rain began. Then the Flood came, and the rain fell forty days and forty nights.

Are we preachers of righteousness? Are our thoughts, words, and deeds eloquent for God? It is not necessary to stand up to preach at street corners as some fanatics think. If S. Paul began to preach immediately after his conversion, we must remember that he was a clever and educated man. What God needs is the witness of consistent lives.

"Let your conversation (*i.e.*, manner of life, R.V.) be as it becometh the Gospel of Christ" (Phil. i. 27). We are the salt of the earth, the light of the world.

4. The Flood is a type of Baptism. The water of the Flood saved Noah who was in the ark; the water of Baptism saves us who are in the ark of Christ's Church (see 1 Peter iii. 20, 21). But further, as the water was the instrument of salvation to Noah, it was also the instrument of destruction to the wicked; both these ideas are made use of in the Baptismal Office, where the ark is the "Church," the water "the waves of this troublesome world," and the shore "the land of everlasting life." Noah and his family were saved from the destruction of the Flood; every baptized person is saved from the destruction of original sin; but as Ham turned out badly afterwards, so, alas, do many of the baptized.

CHAPTER VI., Sec. 2.

Monday.

THE PUNISHMENT OF ADAM.
Gen. III.

NOTES:—

1. Adam's sin in its result is well known to the experience of us all. In its nature it is fixed in our memories by the first lines of Milton's great poem—

> "Of man's first disobedience, and the fruit
> Of that forbidden tree, whose mortal taste
> Brought death into the world, and all our woe,
> With loss of Eden, till our greater Man
> Restore us, and regain the blissful seat,
> Sing, heavenly Muse."

As disobedience was the first sin, so it is the root of every sin; for every sin breaks some commandment; every sin is a wrong done and a right left undone. We cannot say what might have happened if Adam had never sinned, but we do know that, terrible as are the effects of that sin, God over-ruled them for good:—"Where sin abounded grace did much more abound" (Rom. v. 20). And it is supposed that the righteousness we can win through Christ, transcends original righteousness that we lost in Adam.

2. The devil, our great spiritual enemy, is called from his cunning craftiness the "old serpent" (Rev. xii. 9), because "the serpent was more subtle than any beast of the field." In the same way Herod is called a "fox," and for much the same reason (Luke xiii. 32). Herod was not actually a fox, but only like one; the devil did not metamorphose himself into a serpent. As far as we know the serpent has always crawled on its belly, but after the Fall it became a sign, like the rainbow became a sign after the Flood. The old Masters thoroughly understood this, and when they painted pictures of the scene they treated the serpent merely as a symbol and often drew it with a human head.

3. In 1 Tim. ii. 14 there is a startling statement. "Adam was not deceived, but the woman being deceived was in the transgression!" A deception was practised on the woman, being taken in she sinned; Adam, on the other hand, sinned willingly, with his eyes open as it were; and though they were both severely punished, the sentence on Eve was heavier than the sentence on Adam, contrary to our expectation. Why was it? And if Adam was not deceived why did he sin at all? Milton seems to give the correct solution in saying that Adam's motive for eating was love for his wife; he would

not be separated from her even in evil; she had raised a barrier between them, so he joined her in the transgression. This also accounts for his lighter punishment; it is better to love amiss than not to love at all. Moreover, to her sin of disobedience she added the sin of deception, for she attempted, though unsuccessfully, to deceive her husband. This last point illustrates the fact that one sin often involves another, which follows quickly in its wake.

4. As regards the position of woman, it is clear that one of two partners must, of necessity, take the second place, and it has fallen to the lot of woman to do so. She ranks second to her husband, though it does not follow that she is inferior to him; in fact many men acknowledge a superiority in speaking of their wife as their "better half," and many women are really superior to many men. In the earlier ages of the world, and still amongst savage tribes, the position of woman is anything but delectable; Christianity, but not civilization, has ameliorated her lot, and raised her in the social scale, so that if she is able she can make good an equality with man. Still she must take second place. It is so at the font, where boys are baptized before girls. It is so at the altar step where boys are confirmed before girls. It is so at those churches where the sexes are divided, and the men sit on the right hand. Moreover women must keep silent in church (1 Cor. xiv. 34). They

The Punishment of Adam. 135

may of course join in hymns, responses, etc., *i.e.*, in the common service, but must take no leading part. Therefore mixed choirs, and so-called "angel" choirs, are an abomination, nor are solos in church by female operatic singers and others permitted.

5. There is another verse much to our purpose (1 Tim. ii. 15)—"She shall be saved through the Child-bearing." Child-bearing, which was the instrument of her punishment, was made also the instrument of her salvation, and so answered the end of all just punishment. Women share equally with men the blessings of the Incarnation, and on the same conditions, " if they continue in faith, and love, and sanctification, with sobriety."

6. As God was going to turn evil into good, when He inflicted the punishment He foretold the release. "The LORD God said unto the serpent . . . I will put enmity between thee and the woman, and between thy seed and her seed; it shall bruise thy head, and thou shalt bruise his heel." This was the dawn of Hope, in the light of which man lived, as it brightened through the ages, until "the Sun of Righteousness arose with healing in His wings."

7. Of the coming Messiah we are told, much to our surprise, that Adam was a type or figure (Rom. v. 14). Type is here used in its wider sense, and Christ is compared to Adam rather by way of contrast than by way of similarity. In Adam we partake of human nature, in Christ of the divine.

From Adam we receive sin, from Christ righteousness. From Adam we inherit death, from Christ life. "As in Adam all die, even so in Christ shall all be made alive" (1 Cor. xv. 22). Adam was the destroyer, Christ is the Restorer. Adam was the head of the human race, but fell, Christ in becoming the second Adam took his place. Even the locality is said to be the same, and therefore, according to one of the symbolic legends, Christ was crucified where Adam was buried, and at the foot of the Cross we often see his skull. "He . . . went forth into a place called the place of a skull . . . where they crucified Him" (John xix. 17). Thus the punishment of the first sin passed upon all the descendants of the first sinner, and was felt even by Him Who knew no sin.

CHAPTER VI., Sec. 3.

Tuesday.

THE PUNISHMENT OF JOSEPH.

Gen. xxxvii. 23 to 29, and xxxix. 20.

Notes :—

1. The misfortunes that befel Joseph, his kidnapping, his sale, his separation from home, and his imprisonment, must be regarded, not altogether as a discipline to prepare him for his future success, but also partly in the aspect of a punishment for his vanity. His famous cloak, and his more famous dreams had a tendency to turn his head, but this weakness in his character was afterwards corrected by his misfortunes. Also he was a tale-bearer, bringing to his father the "evil report" of his brethren : this would never do in a statesman who was to govern an important country, and is a fault that is only eradicated by severity.

2. Vanity is a breach of the first commandment, because it assigns to self a higher place than to God. It is putting self before God. We have nothing to

boast of. "What hast thou that thou didst not receive? Now if thou didst receive it, why dost thou glory, as if thou hadst not received it?" (1 Cor. iv. 7). In Joseph's case the cloak was clearly a gift from his father, and the dreams were vouchsafed by God. He had no ground for presuming on the favour he had found with God and man; when he did so, his brothers hated him, his father rebuked him, and God punished him.

3. Tale-bearing is a breach of the ninth commandment. It injures the reputation of other people; whereas Love does not take account of evil, rejoiceth not in unrighteousness, covereth all things. The tale-bearer, in his microscopic observation of others, forgets to know himself: he sees evil where he might see good: he takes a pleasure in the shortcomings of his neighbour: he is very apt to lie: and he is very near akin to the traitor: he cannot be trusted.

4. If Joseph was lacking in self-command when tempted to think too highly of his honours, or to gratify his taste for gossip; on another trying occasion, when alone with his master's wife, he showed clearly enough that he possessed that quality, which was afterwards to be so highly developed. On that particular occasion he asked a question that we might put to ourselves with advantage, when face to face with temptation—"How can I do this great wickedness, and sin against God?" If we could

only cultivate this splendid power of recollection we should be saved from many tumbles.

5. Joseph is a fine type of Christ.

Joseph means "increase."	"He must increase."
Joseph was a rising man.	Christ was a rising Man.
Joseph went down into Egypt.	Christ went down into Egypt.
Joseph was sold by his brethren.	Christ was sold by Judas.
Joseph was put in the pit.	Christ "descended into hell."
Joseph was taken out of the pit.	Christ rose again.
Joseph was exalted to Pharaoh's right hand.	Christ ascended, and sat on the right hand of God.
Before Joseph heralds cried, "Bow the knee."	"At the Name of Jesus every knee shall bow."
Joseph was Ruler of Egypt.	Christ is King of kings.
Joseph loved a brother.	Christ loved a disciple.
Joseph had a scheme of salvation.	Christ also saves His people from their sins.
Joseph forgave his brothers.	Christ forgave His enemies.

In tracing a type many points of similarity are no doubt rather fanciful, but where a distinct event is involved they are more decided, and seem as if they must be ordered by God, which is surely the case when they are brought forward by writers of the New Testament. When they involve a trait of character they may very well be reproduced in ourselves, as we make progress in the imitation of Christ.

CHAPTER VI., Sec. 4.

Wednesday.

THE PUNISHMENT OF PHARAOH.

Exodus xiv.

NOTES :—

1. When Moses attended the Egyptian Court, on the summons of the king after the ninth plague, it was for the last time, and the king said, " See my face no more." Nearly 4,000 years have passed since then, and photographs of this king are sold in the London shops! and his very face can be looked upon in the Museum at Gizeh. There are the three great kings of the nineteen dynasty—Seti I., Ramses II. the Great, the Sesostris of the Greeks, he of the oppression, and Marenptah, the Pharaoh of the Exodus. Some idea of the splendid state of these kings may be formed at the Soane Museum, Lincoln's Inn Fields, where the magnificent alabaster sarcophagus, or chest for containing the coffin, may be seen. It is cut from a single block, carved and painted, and for it the British Museum offered £10,000!

2. The final punishment of Pharaoh, recorded in the chapter chosen for to-day, involved many important events.

(a) The institution of the Passover. The great king is a dried and wizen mummy, little more than a name to most of us, occupying his niche in history; but the ordinance of the Passover, celebrated first with such haste in the huts of the fugitive nation, has survived. It gives the name to Easter among all Christian nations except ourselves. The central point of the ritual was the lamb. This lamb was first a sacrifice and then a feast. As such it is perhaps the most famous of types. It is a symbol of Christ. It was without blemish, Christ was sinless. Not a bone of the lamb was to be broken, not a bone of Christ was broken at Crucifixion. It was offered to God, so was Christ. The people fed on the sacrifice. Christ gave us His Body and Blood to eat and drink. Those Israelites who observed its rules escaped destruction, and those Christians who make devout Communions receive the gift of life. Like the Passover the Eucharist is both a continual Sacrifice and a Feast.

Further, the Israelites were to be ready with an answer to the question, "What mean ye by this service?" The question presupposes thorough instruction on the part of adults, and eagerness to learn on the part of the children. This very reasonable state of things commanded so long ago has not yet been attained. We may ask how many Christians could give an intelligible account of the leading ideas of the Eucharist? And how many children are brought up with a desire for information? Their frame of mind is rather, "I don't care to learn." Knowledge of the Eucharist should be made a test of faith, and attendance at Eucharist a test of practice in every parish. It is an admirable test of the efficiency of the teacher, and the progress of the taught. This is the edification of the Church, which it is a thousand pities to sacrifice to mere number. Quality should never give way to quantity.

(*b*) The consecration of the first-born. Everyone and everything belongs to God. The consecration of the first-born was an acknowledgment of this. It was fulfilled in Christ, Who was "the first-born among many brethren," and in Him we find our consecration, as "the Church of the first-born."

(*c*) The Passage of the Red Sea. This is a perfect type of Baptism. Behind was Egypt, or the world. Before was the desert, or the pilgrimage through life. Still further ahead was the Promised Land, or Heaven. There was the passage of the sea. That is Baptism. All the people passed through; infants are baptized. They went down into the bed of the sea, they passed along the bed, and emerged on the other side; so we descend, as it were, into the water of Baptism, remain a brief interval below the water, and rise again. The Israelites were in a state of salvation, so are the Baptized. Many of the Israelites perished in the wilderness for their sins; and many of the Baptized will likewise perish.

3. At the final interview between Moses and Ramses the Great, the King made a strange request, "Bless me also" (xii. 32). We may contrast this with the prayer of Esau. Both men were dazzled with power. Ramses with the power of Moses, and its extraordinary manifestations in his kingdom; Esau with the authority and influence that the blessing was to bring with it. Neither cared for the blessing itself, but only for the advantage. Esau was blessed, but we do not read that Moses granted the request of Ramses. In the end, Esau repented, as we have seen, while Pharaoh hardened his heart.

CHAPTER VI., Sec. 5.

Thursday.

THE PUNISHMENT OF ISRAEL.

Num. xxi. 4 to 10, and Psalm lxxviii. 12 to 42.

Notes:—

1. The order "to compass the land of Edom" was given because the Edomites were a kindred nation, descendants of Esau. They did not prove themselves very friendly; they would not allow the migrating people to pass through their country, but hostilities were avoided by a circuitous march, and did not break out till a later period.

2. The people, contrasting the wilderness with Egypt, were discouraged, and, remembering the plenty in their scarceness, grumbled. They trusted neither God nor Moses, though his skilfulness as a leader might have been apparent, confirmed as it had been by his startling miracles. The same ethical process is witnessed in all ages. Our Lord said, "If they believe not Moses and the prophets, neither will they be persuaded, though one rose from the dead" (Luke xvi. 31).

If men have no faith in God, we can have no ground of faith in them. In so far as a man proves himself faithless, he proves himself Christless. To betray another is a terrible sin. A traitor is the most abandoned villain. High treason is rightly punished with death. We execrate Judas. Yet his spirit is abroad.

3. Manna was a type of the Bread of Life, which came down from Heaven. In Psalm lxxviii. 11 it is said, in the exuberance of the imagination of an Eastern poet, that "man did eat angels' food." We may find an explanation in the margin—"every one did eat the bread of the mighty," *i.e.*, the bread that makes strong. It seems utterly unreal, and far-fetched, to speak of the Body of Christ as "angels' food," according to the expression of many hymns, because, the explanation being so remote, the words are likely to mislead. The danger of unreality is always very great, without increasing it by artificial means.

4. "Our soul loatheth this light food." Does not this represent the attitude of mind of those people who never make their communion? They despise, they reject, they dislike the means of grace. They murmur, they will not trust. The result is fatal, for not only will God punish them in the future, but He withdraws Himself in the present. This is sadly but beautifully expressed by the Psalmist, "They limited the Holy One of Israel" (lxxviii. 41, A.V.). The same

thing was also said of our Lord, and for the same cause—" He did not many mighty works there, because of their unbelief" (Matt. xiii. 58). What would not God do for us if we only permitted Him to carry out all His gracious purposes! When we prevent Him doing so we stand in the way of our own progress, we do not recognize our best interest.

5. "Moses prayed for the people," at their own request. The duty of intercession lies upon us all. It is much neglected. Prayer is too selfish. We forget the force of the plural in the Paternoster. We should pray for all sorts and conditions of men. Christianity is a social religion. Our welfare depends upon the welfare of others. If we ask only for the blessings of the individual, we are likely to miss the blessings of the community. Intercession is a special priestly duty, which we, who are "a royal priesthood," are bound to cultivate. Moses was not a priest, yet Moses prayed for the people, and with success.

6. The brazen serpent. We can very well imagine that a great many folks never looked at the brazen serpent after all. Those who did were miraculously healed. The condition of the cure lay in exercising the very virtue in which they had been deficient—trust in God. Henceforth the serpent became a relic, which was permitted to be kept, till it became an object of superstitious veneration, and then in the reign of Hezekiah it was destroyed.

This serpent is instanced by our Lord as a type of

Himself. It is a type of the Crucifixion. "As Moses lifted up the serpent in the wilderness, even so must the Son of Man be lifted up," and for the same reason, "that whosoever believeth in Him should not perish, but have eternal life." But not only was Christ lifted up on the Cross, He is also lifted up over the altar at the Eucharist; and again there is life to him that believeth. "I, if I be lifted up . . . will draw all men unto Me" (John xii. 32).

> "Enough! for see, with dim association
> The tapers burn, the odorous incense feeds
> A fiery flame; the solemn Mass proceeds;
> The priest bestows the appointed consecration;
> And, while the Host is raised, its elevation
> An awe and supernatural feeling breeds:
> And all the people bow their heads like reeds
> To a soft breeze, in lowly adoration."
> —*Wordsworth (adapted)*.

CHAPTER VI., Sec. 6.

Friday.

THE PUNISHMENT OF BETHEL.

2 Kings ii. 23, 24.

Notes :—

1. It is impossible to help feeling a certain amount of satisfaction in this story. That feeling is, of course, wrong, for in it lurks the latent idea of revenge, which is so very sweet to man. We can hear Christ saying to us so gently, yet so firmly, "Ye know not what manner of spirit ye are of" (Luke ix. 55). In Dumas' famous story of Monte Christo the Count plans an elaborate revenge, but just at the moment of accomplishment the Almighty interposes by punishing the victim himself, and at the same time teaching the Count that "Vengeance is Mine, I will repay, saith the Lord!" (Rom. xii. 19). But the vengeance of God is not subject to the weakness of the vengeance of man, for it is not swayed by feelings however righteous; it is entirely passionless; also being directed by Omniscience it fits the case exactly.

2. How we can picture the scene! Elisha is on the high road near the city; the children are out for a holiday, and seeing an old man of weird appearance think that he is fair game, and call after him, "Go up, thou bald head! Go up!" This is the ribaldry of the streets. It is of daily occurrence. "Hair cut!" "Hair cut!" "Keep your hair on!" are familiar expressions amongst ourselves, and contain about as much sense. They are foolish, because even if they once had a point it has been lost by countless repetition; and they are devilish because meant to provoke. They are condemned by the law of murder, read in its wider sense, which stands at the head of the second tablet as the first duty we owe our neighbour.

It is one of the signs of the times, and a very terrible sign too. It is a mark of a vicious and degenerate society, when "the child shall behave himself proudly against the ancient" (Isa. iii. 5). The insolence of the children reveals the weakness of the parents, who fail to exercise their legitimate control. Humility is good for us all—"to order myself lowly and reverently to all my betters," betters in age and experience, betters in position and wealth, betters in intellect and virtue. Submission is good for us all—"to submit myself to all my governors, teachers, spiritual pastors, and masters." These virtues are considered much out of date; every man does that which is right in his own eyes, restrained

The Punishment of Bethel. 151

only by the tyranny of power and propriety.

3. Reverence and politeness are kindred duties that we owe respectively to God and man. Genuine politeness springs from that consideration for others which is taught through the Incarnation. The decay of manners has accompanied the decay of religion. A certain formal politeness may be acquired in so-called society, but is a hollow sham. The world of fashion has been called, by Marie Corelli, "the world of mockery," where every better instinct of human nature guided by Christianity, is insulted and outraged.

4. Only one sort of punishment is effective. The fool mocks at reason; the heartless laugh at kindness; the profane ridicule religion; the only possible cure is the brute force of the bear; no other is understood. This force should be strictly applied by those in authority, to eradicate the evil in young people. "The Law" is of the nature of brute force, men are said to fall into its "clutches," from which there is no release until the penalty is paid; when in its power man is helpless. Under the vengeance of God man is also helpless. Now it is from this power that Christ came to save us, and it will be with this power that Christ comes to judge us.

5. Elisha, who received not double the spirit of Elijah, but the double portion of the first-born, is a remarkable type of Christ, "in Whom dwelleth the fulness of the Godhead bodily" (Col. ii. 9); and the

type does not fail in this particular. It is true Christ rebuked His disciples for wishing to call down fire from Heaven, even though it was to avenge an insult offered to their Master; but it was from no easy-going, good-natured tolerance for sin. The occasion was not ripe. There will be no hesitation in passing sentence on the damned; with unrelenting voice He will say, "Depart from Me, ye cursed, into eternal fire, prepared for the devil and his angels" (Matt. xxv. 41). God is Love, all tender, all compassionate, but when the sinner, in the hardness of his heart, has passed that point in his career when he is untouched by tenderness, and uncompelled by compassion, then, just because God is Love, He will be stern and merciless.

CHAPTER VI., SEC. 7.

𝔖𝔞𝔱𝔲𝔯𝔡𝔞𝔶.

THE PUNISHMENT OF CHRIST.

ISA. LII. 12 to LIII. end.

NOTES :—

1. There is a strange idea abroad in the minds of many people that Christ died "instead" of us. One moment's consideration should be enough to dispel such an idea for ever, did not mistakes die hard. There are two sorts of death—death of the body, and death of the soul; or, as we may put it, physical death, and spiritual death. We are still subject to physical death; therefore it is not physical death that Christ suffered *instead* of us: and as to spiritual death, God forbid that He suffered that. Again, the same expression "for" (ὑπέρ) is used both of the death and of the resurrection of Christ; therefore, in whatever sense He died for us, He also rose for us: God forbid that He rose instead of us! (see 2 Cor. v. 15). "Who for their sakes died and rose again." The conclusion is that the word "for" is used in its other signification, "on behalf of." Hence we get

rid, for ever, of the monstrous idea of vicarious suffering, and with it of vicarious punishment.

2. The death of Christ, which only became possible through the Incarnation, may be considered under three of the most remarkable words used in connection with it.

(*a*) Propitiation. This means making gracious. It is a very old idea, common to all religions, by which the devotees attempt, with sacrifices, to make their angry God look favourably upon them. God the Son, however, did not offer Himself as a Victim to appease the wrath of God the Father. God, looking down with Divine compassion, wished to make Himself gracious in the eyes of man, and to that end adopted sacrifice as the means, because men understood it.

(*b*) Atonement, or Reconciliation. God and man were separated by sin. Each was angry with the other. God was justly angry with man for his wrong doing; and man, being foolishly angry with God, committed acts of rebellion, *i.e.*, sins, against Him. Any process, therefore, which was a means of bringing God and man together again, by getting rid of the separating cause, would be a reconciliation or atonement, *i.e.*, according to the admitted derivation, "at-one-ment," the making at one.

(*c*) Redemption. Christ redeemed us, bought us back for the glory of God. That we might enjoy salvation, life, happiness, He bought us by a career of suffering—in a word, by His blood. In order to understand the process we have but to consider what was once an ordinary transaction of life. A man travels; he falls into the hands of brigands, who take him prisoner, and demand a ransom; his friends raise a sum of money, send it to him, and by means of it he obtains his freedom. In the same way we fall into the hands of the devil, and Christ, at the cost of bloodshed, provides us with the means of escape, *i.e.*, with grace to resist our enemy and keep the law of holiness.

3. How does this happen? We are attracted to Christ by what He has done for us. Without actually bestowing upon us the Holy Spirit, God causes this attraction, which, in other language, is termed our "call"; God causes us to wish for, and to ask for, the means of leading a new life. This means is the ransom. This means is obtained only in consequence of the shedding of Christ's blood, which is said, by another figure of speech, to cleanse us from all sin. This means is called grace, and grace is obtained chiefly through the Sacraments, which are outward and visible signs for our bodies, conveying the inward and spiritual grace to our souls.

4. Means of grace are both mental and sacramental. Means of grace are chiefly sacramental, for it is the sacraments which are with us from the cradle to the grave, it is the sacraments which provide for every emergency of life. Means of grace

are slightly mental, for prayer, study of Scripture, and meditation are helps in the spiritual life; but the man who relied on these last alone would be very foolish; he would be like a fellow who, observing that the blind got on very well without their eyes, put out his own!

The most important of the mental means of grace is "spiritual communion"—but that only to a certain extent, for it cannot be made unless the Eucharist is said. It is only mentioned here to make the statement quite complete; but for an explanation of it the reader is referred to some manual of devotion, such as "Before the Altar." We need only add that it is supplemental to actual Communion, and is not to be habitually used instead of it.

5. The suffering of Christ can only be regarded as a punishment in so far as, wishing to show His boundless Love, He submitted Himself, being sinless, to what was the punishment of sin. By His death He won those thanks and that acceptance with God referred to by S. Peter, in 1 Ep. ii. 19, 20, and which are won by the patient man who suffers wrongfully, and is buffeted for well-doing.

CHAPTER VII., Sec. 1.

Palm Sunday.

THE DAY OF HOSANNAS.
Matt. xxi. 1 to 18.

Notes :—

1. At last we come to Holy Week, when the tragedy of our Lord's life deepens to its close, when the story is told with great minuteness of detail, so that we can almost follow exactly what He did day by day. It seems a pity that the Gospels in the Missal are not arranged on this plan, giving, as far as possible, a succinct diary of the last days, instead of repeating at great length the different accounts of the Passion. It would be most instructive, as showing how the Divine Master employed His time just before death. This is the narrative which is to occupy our thoughts until Easter.

2. Six days before the Passover Jesus came to Bethany. This was on the Friday evening, a little after the Sabbath had begun. At Bethany he was entertained at supper by a very ungracious host, Simon, a Pharisee, who is called the leper, but must have been cured.

3. Sunday. The Day of Hosannas. Our Lord would go up to town, up to the Capital, up to the Holy City, as afterwards He would go up to Heaven, and as His followers have to follow Him beneath their excelsior banner of Love (Cant. ii. 4). When they arrived at the ascent of the Mount of Olives, at the boundary of the parishes, if we may say so, of Bethany and Bethphage, He sent two of His disciples forward into the village, where a friend of His lived who had a colt, which he would be willing to lend if the disciples said, " The Lord hath need of him." This is one of those beautiiul sayings capable of spiritual application to ourselves,—the Lord hath need of us! Is there anything that the Creator lacks ? Yes! our hearts. God often supplies our wants, herein we are privileged to supply His. The colt was brought, a young thing that had never been used in the service of the world. They set Him thereon, and so He rode meekly, humbly forward to meet His death, confident in the success of His life and the final triumph of His principles. A crowd came forth to meet Him, a crowd followed Him. It was a state entry into Jerusalem. Never did He permit Himself to be so nearly acknowledged King as when He was accompanied to the Capital by that clamorous multitude, bearing palm branches and crying hosanna. Every procession is a type of life, and this procession, not only makes a precedent for every procession at church, but is also especially

commemorated year by year at the procession, benediction, and distribution of palms on the Sunday before Easter. A procession is an excellent plan of stirring our devotion, as it woke the enthusiasm of the people to cry, "Blessed is He that cometh in the name of the Lord, hosanna in the highest,"—hosanna!

On the way to the City He paused to weep over it, sad in the midst of the acclamations of His followers. He wept at the coming destruction, He wept at the fatality of the siege, He wept because the citizens did not, and would not, know the things belonging to their peace. If repentance excites joy in Heaven, sin must excite grief, how great then must be the grief of the Saviour when He looks down upon the cities of the modern world, which, like Jerusalem, have rejected Him, and practically ceased to be Christian cities at all, having crucified their Lord afresh! It is one of the saddest incidents in a sad life, the tears of Jesus falling at the thought of the reckless folly and the hard stubborness of those He came to save; Love wounded in its tenderest affection; Love disappointed in its dearest wish; Love spurned in its efforts; Love sobbing at its rejection.

We have all seen how a hen gathers her chicks beneath her wing; so would our Lord have gathered His people, if only they would have confided in His wish. His anxiety to protect, and His zeal to defend, knew no bounds. Those who love and study animals will best appreciate this beautiful figure of Eastern speech.

When He reached the Temple He found it a scene of great disorder, and, in the enthusiasm of the moment, He drove forth the merchants and money-changers. Once before, at the beginning of His career, He had done the same thing. The difference between these two occasions is marked by the difference of His description of the state of affairs. On the first occasion He said, " Make not My Father's House an house of merchandise " (John ii. 16); on the second occasion things had gone from bad to worse, and He said, "Ye have made it a den of thieves." The priests and scribes were indignant, but helpless ; and in spite of their remonstrance the choir boys cried, Hosanna !

A deputation of Greeks sought an interview; they came to Philip, who took them to Andrew, and he, who had already brought others to Christ, introduced them to the Royal Presence. It was the first meeting of Europeans with our Lord, represented by individuals of the most intellectual race. The importance of the occasion was marked by a voice from Heaven, which the Jews seem not to have heard, and by a memorable saying of our Lord, " I, if I be lifted up from the earth, will draw all men unto Me." This is true of the crucifixion, and it is also true of the elevation of the Host. Only let the Real Presence be taught to and understood by the people, only let the Host be raised for worship, and distributed more frequently for reception, and our Churches will again be crowded as they were in the days when Sacramental truth was more fully held, and the people will not let their voice be silent in the Hosannas of the Eucharist.

CHAPTER VII., Sec. 2.

Monday.

THE DAY OF PARABLES.

MATT. xxi. 18 to xxii. 15.

NOTES :—

1. Coming again to Jerusalem, in the neighbourhood of Bethphage, "the house of figs," He saw a fig tree full of leaves, but when He looked for fruit there was none. A fig tree was made the subject of a remarkable miracle, as it had previously been of a significant parable, which we will consider first. "A certain man had a fig tree planted in his vineyard; and he came and sought fruit thereon, and found none. Then said he to the dresser of his vineyard, Behold, these three years I came seeking fruit on this fig tree, and find none; cut it down! why cumbereth it the ground? And he, answering, said unto him, Lord, let it alone this year also, till I shall dung about it: and if it have fruit, well: and if not, then after that thou shalt cut it down" (Luke xiii. 6-10). The interpretation is clear: the Jewish nation was the fig tree in the Lord's vineyard; the Lord came

each several year of His ministry looking for fruits of acceptance; He came into His own country, and His own people received Him not: at last He condemned the nation, most reluctantly, to be cut off; yet, before the final destruction of Jerusalem, another forty years was allowed to elapse, during which the Apostles attempted the conversion of the people, and failed. This teaching was now enforced by a miracle.

We gather from the miracle that performance, which should match promise, often falls short of it, and is punished. Europe professes Christianity, but is Europe Christian? Surely it is time to take S. Paul's warning, which he conveyed in the similar parable of the wild olive. The Jews, said he, were like an olive; all the branches were cut off; and the Gentiles, the wild olive, were grafted on to the original stock. Then comes the warning. "Be not high-minded, but fear: for if God spared not the natural branches, take heed lest He also spare not thee" (Rom. xi. 13-22).

In a lighter vein we may add—

> "Words are like leaves,
> And where they most abound
> Much fruit of sense beneath
> Is rarely found."
> —*Pope*.

2. The Parable of the two Sons shows the value of repentance and the worthlessness of empty pro-

fession. The first son had some vigour about him, declaring openly, "I will not"; the second displayed a provoking acquiescence that was disappointing in its result. These are but types of characters that are constantly met with in the world,—opposition and indifference. It is far easier to deal with a candid opponent than with a listless fellow who, quite uninterested, seeks to please by words, but is unconcerned about deeds. A few examples may be taken out of hundreds:—In society, the guest who disappoints his host. In business, the trader who meets you with bland smiles, and treats you to mean tricks. In religion, the Sunday School teacher who undertakes a class and neglects it: or the boy who eagerly joins some guild, and often stays away from the meetings. Lack of interest has destroyed many a fair prospect, and shows how necessary it is to stir up the gift that is in us, and to pray the collect for the last Sunday after Trinity.

3. Next, follow three parables all with the same teaching,—the rejection and punishment of the Jews. The Wicked Husbandmen; the Rejected Corner Stone; and the Marriage of the King's Son. In these parables we may note our Lord's method of attack. The day for the statement of positive truth had gone by, the time for denunciation had come. Though it is not our custom to speak in parables we must remember that their meaning was perfectly plain to an Eastern mind. Our Lord now wished

either to rouse them to conversion by alarm, or to drive them to extremities by anger. His words had the latter effect, "they sought to lay hold of Him."

Again, our Lord as God knew that His hour approached, as Man He could foresee that His end was near by the signs of the times, yet with what wonderful calmness and confidence He met His death; His mind perfectly clear, His courage unabated. In His discourses, what wealth of illustration, what power of language, what boldness of thought, what directness of attack.

Lastly, He closes the day with the pathetic admission that "many are called, but few are chosen," which throws the responsibility on ourselves, and should set any thoughtful man thinking about the answer he intends to make, on which his eternal welfare will depend.

CHAPTER VII., Sec. 3.

Tuesday.

THE DAY OF QUESTIONS.
MATT. XXII. 15 to end.

NOTES :—

1. The effect of the curse on the fig-tree, of which we read yesterday, was not seen before this morning, though it is recorded by S. Matthew as if it were an instantaneous result. His word "presently," or "immediately," signifies in an unusually short space of time. He wished to present the story as a whole, therefore he told it altogether, instead of referring to it twice. S. Mark gives a fuller account; he records the very words of the curse, and says it was S. Peter who next morning called attention to the effect. When no fruits of the Spirit are produced then we ought to point out the fact, and by asking the first question of the Day of Questions, "How did the fig-tree immediately wither away?" (R.V.) enquire the cause to learn the remedy.

2. Verse 15 shows how the Pharisees employed the interval between Monday evening and Tuesday

morning in concocting catch questions, "that they might ensnare Him in His talk." All three questions must have been due to them, for it could scarcely have been by accident that the Sadducees put their question on the same day.

3. The union of Pharisees and Herodians was an exceedingly cunning combination. The Pharisees were the religious and national party, who proudly declared, "We be Abraham's seed, and were never in bondage to any man." The Herodians were the political and diplomatic party, who believed the national life depended quite as much on the goodwill of the Romans as upon the observation of the Mosaic Law. "Is it lawful to give tribute unto Cæsar, or not?" they asked. If He answered "Yes," He displeased the Pharisees, who would immediately denounce Him to the multitude as the enemy of religion, and He would lose His influence with them. Moreover, the multitude, already objecting to the Roman occupation, would be easily roused to violence by the submission recommended. If He answered "No," He offended the Herodians, who would look upon Him as the enemy of His country, and would perhaps denounce Him to the civil authority, by way of removing Him from public life; also the multitude would be wildly excited, and encouraged in the hope of a successful rebellion.

His penetrating intellect pierced their craft. He lifted the question from its original level, as applying to the particular circumstances of those who asked it, and drew out the underlying principle, that authority must be respected, that Church and State must be obeyed, that all must have their dues, whether tribute, or honour, or custom, in a word, that there is a double duty to God and man.

4. The Sadducees came forward and fared no better than their enemies. Not believing in the resurrection, they put before Him a complicated case for solution. Again He raised the question from the particular to the general. While asserting in the strongest possible terms the doctrine of a life hereafter, He quietly avoided satisfying their idle curiosity about any particular case. "They erred, not knowing the power of God" to deal with altered conditions of existence. Again, "they erred, not knowing the Scriptures," even the Books of Moses, the very Scriptures upon which they laid so much stress, they had failed in their understanding of the famous proclamation, "I am the God of Abraham, and the God of Isaac, and the God of Jacob." He only answered their question directly, in as far as He stated, that in the world to come there would be no sex relationship. As Love is independent of sex, so is Life. The multitude were astonished, and one of the Scribes exclaimed, "Master, Thou hast well said" (Luke xx. 39).

5. The third question of the Scribe, who was a Pharisee, was the most honest of all the questions,

and contained no trap. The questioner was more or less sincere. But, notwithstanding, it was a question that tempted, that was put as a further test of our Lord's ingenuity. "Which is the great Commandment in the Law?" Again the answer was admirable. The first is that which commands the duty to God, and the second is that which commands the duty to one's neighbour. The latter is second because it depends on the first, and is "like" unto it, because they both depend on Love. The sequel to this question and answer is found only in S. Mark xii. 32, 33, 34. The Scribe replies discreetly, and Jesus says, "Thou art not far from the Kingdom of God." This put an end to all further questions. The Queen of Sheba had put many subtle questions to Solomon, but they were from admiration of his wisdom, and she expected the answers. The Jews put their insidious questions to Christ from envy of His wisdom, and they hoped He would not be able to answer. The result was just the opposite to what they intended. He gained immensely in the estimation of the multitude, while they lost ground by contrast, for they appeared both malicious and foolish; and they were next to appear ignorant.

6. Quoting from Psalm cx., admittedly Messianic, our Lord asks how David can address his own son as Lord, a thing utterly inconceivable according to Jewish ideas. The answer is, because He was God. Christ was acknowledged to be the son of David; if

the Pharisees allowed He was God also, they must accept Him as the promised Messiah; they preferred to take refuge in silence. Thus their discomfiture was complete.

7. On this day also the Pharisees were denounced; the woman cast her two mites into the treasury; the destruction of Jerusalem and the end of the world were foretold; and the parables of the Ten Virgins and the Talents were spoken.

CHAPTER VII., Sec. 4.

Wednesday.

THE DAY OF RETIREMENT.
Matt. xxiv. and xxv.

NOTES :—

1. After our Lord's arrival in the neighbourhood of Jerusalem, six days before the Passover (John xii. 1), He had entered the City daily in the morning to teach in the Temple (Luke xix. 47, and xxi. 38), and at night He left the City, either to encamp on the Mount of Olives (Luke xxi. 37), or to stay at Bethany (Matt. xxi. 17), perhaps at the house of His friend Lazarus, where He had stayed and supped on the first night. On Tuesday He "departed from the Temple" for the last time (Matt. xxiv. 1), after having been shown round by the Apostles, and having foretold its destruction.

2. As He sat on the Mount of Olives, Peter, James, John, and Andrew found opportunity to ask Him privately when His prophecies would be fulfilled (Mark xiii. 3). He enlarged upon what He had said before, and concluded with a message to the Church,

"And what I say unto you, I say unto all, Watch!" (Mark xiii. 37). We may take it, therefore, that He passed this day of retirement in spiritual exercises and practical discourses, to prepare Himself and His disciples for the final tragedy.

3. A public man must be able to retire from time to time from the arena of public life, into the calm of the domestic circle, until at last, at the end of his career, he retires altogether. Every one wants a holiday. Most people appreciate a quiet day at the seaside or in the country. We sometimes fly from society and avoid company. These wants are but various manifestations of the necessity of being alone. The body requires it; the soul demands it. Private devotion is no less needful than public worship; they are twins that may not be separated to the soul's health. We may be quite sure that if a man neglects the services of the Church he also neglects the religion of the home, and, if he never prays in his own house, his prayers at Church won't be worth much.

> "By all means use sometimes to be alone.
> Salute thyself: see what thy soul doth wear.
> Dare to look in thy chest; for 'tis thine own:
> And tumble up and down what thou find'st there."
> —*Geo. Herbert.*

4. When alone what shall we do? We must not dream our opportunity away; we must be practical, not vague. We should pray more vehemently than we are able to do at Church, and more particularly;

we should enter into detail, we should intercede, we should agonize. We should read Scripture to learn its letter, and study it to discover its treasure, and acquire its spirit. We should have some simple manual from which to gather at least the outlines of Catholic theology. During Lent we might go through some book of spiritual exercises. We should sum up carefully the results of our life, and make well-arranged plans for the future, so that time may become to us at once more useful and more pleasurable. We should hold a most strict examination of heart; we should sit in judgment on self. And lastly, though work is the best preparation for death, still we should sometimes turn our thoughts to our latter end, as well as contemplate the mysteries of immortality.

Whatever may be said for and against Quiet Days and Retreats, they, at any rate, serve one very useful purpose, in urging the importance, and encouraging the cultivation, of the inner life of holiness, which it is the special office of the Holy Spirit to create, but which is somewhat neglected amid the many distractions of the age.

Life is more eventful than it was; who shall say whether it is more godly? Now that we can move about more quickly from place to place we have not so much spare time on our hands as our forefathers; therefore we should make the best use of what remains. We should aim at quality of work rather than quantity. We should seek friends rather than acquaintances, who consume so much time to such little profit. We should cultivate that strength of character which Christianity requires, and which will stand us in such good stead in the battle of life. It is best done when we are alone with God. We often go to receive the grace of the Sacraments, but how much time do we spend in cherishing and appropriating the gift so as to make it really ours? Solitude stands remote from the busy throng waiting to confer her benediction on the world. Temper, impatience, irritability, waste time and spoil our work; but the man who has been much with self, and God, and nature, is not subject to their evil influence like other men.

Christ often retired from the world, then should not we? Christ often sought refreshment in solitude, then what He valued shall we despise?

5. What was Judas doing on this day? He was preparing his dastardly plan of betrayal; he was receiving the thirty pieces of silver as the first instalment of the price of an innocent life; he was heaping up for himself damnation.

CHAPTER VII., Sec. 5.

Thursday.

THE DAY OF COMMANDMENT.

Matt. xxvi. 26 to 31, and John xiii. 1 to 36.

Notes :—

1. This day is called Maundy Thursday, a title which we may derive from " mandatum," a commandment, and refers to the famous commandment given on this day, " Sacrifice this in remembrance of Me!" Having offered it, feed on it, it is My Body, it is the Bread of Life, it is the vital principle which keeps you alive, it is the force which renews your union with Me and with one another. By doing this you can alone fulfil that old command to love one another, which now for the first time can be kept because it has a new motive. Offer the Sacrifice of the Eucharist for the propitiation of the sins of the world, and in doing it acquire that love which alone can keep the Law, and perform the duties to God and man. Can we neglect our Lord's dying command ?

2. Thus was the Eucharist instituted on that solemn

night before Jesus died for the sins of the world. When He rose it became a thanksgiving, as the Passover had been before it. Its importance demands a day in the Calendar, its jubilant character requires a festival. But as Holy Week is set apart for us to trace the events of the Atonement that had to be made for *our* sins, it is far too sad and solemn to be interrupted by a festival. Therefore the Festival of the Blessed Sacrament had to be postponed to a more suitable day, which the Church found on the Thursday after Trinity Sunday, and named Corpus Christi, or the Festival of the Body of Christ, the Festival of the Real Presence.

3. By the doctrine of the Real Presence is meant that local Presence of our Lord upon the Altar during the Mass. The words of consecration, pronounced by the officiating priest, produce a mysterious change, by which, through the operation of the Holy Spirit, the bread and wine become the Body and Blood. That this change is due to the operation of the Holy Spirit is brought out very beautifully in the form of words used in the Scotch Missal.

Illustrations of so deep a mystery are hard to find. Two have been suggested. Behold yourself in a looking-glass; break the looking-glass, and you see fifty selves, it may be, according to the number of pieces. The Lord is in Heaven; but let the bread be broken on the altars of the churches, and He is in the churches also. Or again, take the parable of the magnet. Magnetize a piece of steel, and it remains a piece of steel, no material difference can be detected, but it possesses a new power. Consecrate the bread, and, as far as the senses can discern, it remains bread, but its nature has been changed, for it has become the Body of Christ.

4. Neglect of the New Commandment accounts for the large number of feeble Christians, and the immense number of those who never go to church at all. There is no reason of much force that will induce men to attend church, if the chief reason of all is omitted. Once teach them the doctrine of the Real Presence, and they are furnished with a sufficient motive. As crowds flock to a Drawing-room when the Queen is there, so crowds would flock to church if they believed the Lord was present.

5. We attend the Eucharist for two purposes. (*a*) For Communion. (*b*) For Worship. Now the Church has ordered fasting reception, therefore we make our communions at an early Eucharist, and because we are fasting the Service is as plain and as short as possible. When we come to worship, however, the Service is on a grander scale, with every adjunct of music and ritual to stir our devotion.

6. There are five parts of the Office, none of which should be lost sight of.

   (*a*) Preparation, for we must not approach so great a mystery thoughtlessly.

(b) Oblation, for we must not come before the Lord empty; He is going to give us a great gift, we must first make our present.

(c) Consecration. This is the central point, without which there would be no Presence, no Sacrifice. It is performed by a duly-appointed priest, who has derived his commission from the Apostles.

(d) Communion, when we receive the Saviour, Who, having already entered the temple of the church, now enters the temple of the heart.

(e) Thanksgiving. We must not forget to return thanks for the benefit we have received. Ingratitude is a bad sin.

CHAPTER VII., Sec. 6.

Friday.

THE DAY OF DEATH.

MATT. XXVII. 27 to 62.

NOTES :—

1. Good Friday. The best Friday that ever was, because the work accomplished on that day was fraught with such momentous results in the salvation of mankind. The solemn day of At-one-ment, the day on which God and man were reconciled, brought together, made at one. As the feast of Sunday is the weekly Easter, so the fast of Friday is the weekly mark of how Christ " suffered under Pontius Pilate, was crucified, dead, and buried." Every effort ought to be made to rescue Good Friday from the profanation of the world. It is a day of meditation not of merriment, a day of devotion not of amusement, a day of religion not of pleasure, a day of seriousness not of frivolity; a solemn fast not a gay feast. We may apply the impressive words of Isaiah about the Sabbath to Good Friday, omitting the joyfulness of the passage, " If thou turn away

thy foot from Good Friday, from doing thy pleasure on my holy day, and call Good Friday the holy of the Lord, honourable; and shalt honour him, not doing thine own ways, nor finding thine own pleasure, nor speaking thine own words; then I will cause thee to ride upon the high places of the earth, and feed thee with the heritage of Jacob thy father" (Isaiah lviii. 13, 14). It is a day for realizing the intensity of the sufferings of Christ, for sympathizing with His agony, and for accepting tearfully the blessed results of His Cross and Passion. It is a day for very deep humiliation on account of our sins which nailed our precious Saviour to the Cross. Even "hot cross buns" should be suppressed, for though a bun does not technically break the fast, it is a little dainty that has no business on a Christian's table.

It is a day of church-going. The churches should be full and the streets empty. The earthly priest suspends his functions on the day on which the great High Priest offered Himself, and therefore the Host is not consecrated on this day alone of all the year. The curtailed Mass of the Pre-sanctified is offered with the reserved elements, the consecration, as the festal part, being omitted.

2. The whole history is so well known that it is scarcely necessary to remind ourselves of it, yet we just state briefly the order of the chief events. (*a*) Preliminary examination before Annas, the ecclesiastical high priest deposed by the Romans,

recorded only by S. John, at which Christ rebuked an officer for contempt of court in striking Him. (*b*) The regular trial before Caiaphas, the political high priest, at which Christ was condemned to death on His own claim to be God. (*c*) The civil trial before Pilate, the Governor, at which He is acquitted; then sent to Herod, as recorded only by S. Luke, and being sent back, is condemned, though innocent, to scourging and death. (*d*) The Crucifixion, 9 a.m. to 3 p.m. Here it may be noted that S. John in xix. 14 reckons his time differently to the other Evangelists, and his sixth hour is 6 a.m. (*e*) Burial.

3. The following are the well-known Stations of the Cross, with thoughts they seem to suggest :—

(1) Jesus is condemned to death.
> Our guilt. Am I innocent? No! I shouted, " Crucify ! "

(2) Jesus receives the Cross.
> Our willingness to suffer.

(3) Jesus falls the first time.
> Humility.

(4) Jesus meets His Blessed Mother.
> Affection.

(5) The Cross is laid on Simon the Cyrenian.
> Our Cross (Matt. xvi. 24).

(6) The face of Jesus is wiped by S. Veronica.
> Truth.

(7) Jesus falls the second time.
> Degradation.

(8) Jesus speaks to the women.
   Repentance. "Weep for yourselves."
(9) Jesus falls the third time.
   Degradation.
(10) Jesus is stripped of His garments.
   Schism. The rude soldiers did not rend the seamless vesture.
(11) Jesus is nailed to the Cross.
   Crucifixion (Gal. v. 24), and mortifying (Col. iii. 5) of the flesh.
(12) Jesus dies upon the Cross.
   Success. "It is finished."
(13) Jesus is taken down from the Cross.
   Care for the dead.
(14) Jesus is laid in the sepulchre.
   Death.

Of these it will be seen that nine are biblical and five legendary; 3 does not seem improbable, after the scourging; 4 is most likely; 6 is clearly allegorical; 7 and 9 appear most improbable, as Simon was carrying the Cross "after" Jesus. The scheme is perhaps useful as fixing the incidents on the mind, and encouraging acts of devotion.

CHAPTER VII., Sec. 7.

Saturday.

THE DAY OF SILENCE.

Matt. xxvii. 62 to end.

NOTES :—

1. In Matt. xxvii. 59 we read that S. Joseph, having received the Body of Jesus, wrapped it in a clean linen "cloth." This is the singular of the word "clothes," now spelt "cloths," which must not be confounded with *clothes*, wearing apparel. The pronunciation of the latter must not be transferred to the former. "Grave clothes" must be pronounced "grave cloths," as it is written in the Revised Version. Yet our ears are annually outraged by the blunders of the clergy. This is a small point, but it has a devotional bearing, for accuracy of speaking leads to accuracy of thinking, which, in its turn, leads to accuracy of living.

2. When our Lord died His Body was put in the grave, and His Soul went to Hades. "He descended into hell," *i.e.*, the unseen world.

His Body was put in the grave. This is no argument against cremation; for His case offers but a very imperfect parallel to ours, since His Body saw no corruption. Nevertheless, the ordinary method does seem the most natural; but brick graves and imperishable coffins are abominations.

His soul went to Hades. While there, He "preached unto the spirits in prison, which aforetime were disobedient" (1 Peter iii. 19). Volumes have been written on this text and the subject it introduces. Our Lord said, "These shalt go away into eternal punishment: but the righteous into eternal life." Whatever sense these words bear in the Gospel they bear in the Athanasian Creed, where alone the Church has pronounced upon the subject. Whatever impression these words may have produced, according to Divine Providence, is quite apart from their real significance, as, of course, thoroughly understood by Him Who spoke them. There is such a thing as the doctrine of reserve: as we don't answer all the questions of a child, so we don't lay the whole truth before the ignorant, but only give them as much as they can bear: milk for babes, strong meat for men. There is such a thing as the wider hope, not to say the comprehensive certainty; but whether this is for the initiated, or the many, may be an open question.

3. The saying of Cleopas on the way to Emmaus well expressed the feeling of the Apostles and their

friends in the interval between the Crucifixion and the Resurrection, "Our rulers . . . crucified Him. But we hoped that it was he which should redeem Israel." Death, sorrow, dejection, hopes crushed, redemption unwrought, utter silence. We cannot very well share the feelings that these men had before the Resurrection, because it is now an accomplished fact, so that this Saturday becomes difficult to keep. Fortunately the day itself is shortened since the first Evensong of every festival is on its eve. The pause enters into the symbol of baptism. The child is dipped into the water, remains for one brief second under the water, and is brought out of the water, in other words it dies, is buried, and rises with Christ. Before Easter it behoves us to do two things, mourn over our sins, and remove everything that will spoil our joy. Now sin, as we have seen, is removed by Confession; and therefore if we confess only once a year, as we should do at least, before Easter is the time to do it.

4. Having called this the Day of Silence, we will consider the worth of silence. The chatter of children is merely an exercise in talking. The silly words of the foolish, and the bad words of the wicked, had better be left unsaid. It is wearying to listen to the one and painful to listen to the other. "Silence is golden," says an old proverb, then how great is the price we pay for speech. Words without thoughts produce no impression. "Think twice

before you speak," is good advice. When Gulliver visited the country of the horses he found they often paused in conversation, that they might always have something worth saying. A reasonable listener is quite as good company as a fluent talker. The man who never listens misses much, especially the good opinion of the person who has something to say. "To everything there is a season . . . a time to keep silence, and a time to speak" (Eccl. iii. 1 and 7). Children should not be too ready to speak, it leads to contradiction and interruption. They should not be allowed to talk in school according to the modern plan, it is a shocking habit that destroys their attention. Men should be ready to speak out, if necessary, what they know to be right.

Talking in Church is irreverent. In children it should be firmly suppressed. Let every one "be silent to the Lord" (Psalm xxxvii. 7). During the Consecration, when the bell rings, a hush should fall upon the congregation; not a whisper, not a sound, not a stir should break upon the solemnity of the moment, for "the Lord is in His holy temple; let all the earth keep silence before Him" (Hab. ii. 20).

We should aim at a just proportion of sound and silence: too much silence makes man stupid, too much sound makes him weary. Sound when musical is pleasant, when noisy is irritating. A day in the country calms a citizen; a day in the city brightens a countryman. If men knew when to keep silent they would not have so many idle words for which to give account, there would not be so much gossip, so much slander, so much tale-bearing. Our tongue should not get the better of our discretion.

Appendix.

NOTE I.

Easter.

V. Christ is risen!
R. Christ is risen indeed!

Having arrived at Easter, our Lenten exercises are over. We hope they have proved useful in stirring up fresh interest in the subjects treated, that they will encourage independent study of the Holy Scriptures, that they will prove useful for more perfect instruction by being repeated in future years.

NOTE II.

The Great Forty Days.

This is the name given to the period between Easter and Ascension. Our Lord employed this time in speaking to the Apostles "of the things pertaining to the Kingdom of God" (Acts i. 3), *i.e.*, the holy Catholic Church, whose constitution He then laid down, and whose organization He sketched.

www.ingramcontent.com/pod-product-compliance
Lightning Source LLC
Chambersburg PA
CBHW020933230426
43666CB00008B/1662